Before We Say
"Goodnight"

Praise for

Before We Say "Goodnight"

━━ ━━ ━

"Hank Frazee's book is right on point with current research that the environment shapes human brain development. Parents telling stories is precisely what helps children to become better people."

ELIZABETH M. KOLVE, MTF, PSY.D.

"There's a wonderful bond forged with our kids when we share our memories by telling them bedtime stories of the unforgettable characters we've known, the exciting experiences we've had, the amazing things we discovered, and the funny things we did as kids. Few things are more important than passing on to the next generation our beliefs and values. In this stunning book, Hank Frazee not only shares his own inimitable bedtime stories but reveals the secret of how to get close to your kids by sharing your own. Every parent and grandparent needs this book. We go around only once with our kids. They long to know us, and telling bedtime stories is a great way to open our hearts to them."

DR. LLOYD JOHN OGILVIE,
Chaplain of the United States Senate, 1995-2003

"Before We Say "Goodnight" is a wonderful and fun learning tool for all parents. As an important alternative to the fairy tale at night, it teaches parents that these moments can turn into an oral history of family adventures from the past. Mr. Frazee gives easy-to-follow instruction that will enable all readers to acquire the skill to be exciting storytellers. A wonderful addition to all family libraries."

GLORIA WATTS, Director of Children's Theatre

"Hank Frazee has written a book about how to tell stories to children. As far as I know, he's the first to do this, which makes his book pretty much invaluable. I too told bedtime tales to my children, but they were mostly my versions of Winnie-the-Pooh and the Doctor Doolittle stories—so inevitably I ran out of ideas fairly quickly. I wish I'd had Hank's book to help me out back then. The concept is terrific, the story ideas inventive, and I applaud him for putting it all down on paper so that parents and guardians (and even wicked uncles like me) will be able to benefit from his marvelous ideas."

IAN OGILVY, Author of the Measle Series

"Hank Frazee's book, Before We Say "Goodnight," is practical and inspirational. Using stories from his own family, Frazee shares his insight on how bedtime can be a special time in every family's day. Using Frazee's methods, bedtime is a place to unpack family stories. It's also a time when you can infuse values with the intention of creating a life-referencing moment between your children and stories of their parents, grandparents, and extended families, as well as connect those stories with the real and imagined. Undoubtedly, the safety of an open and communicative relationship between parent and child is essential for their relational health. I heartily recommend Hank's book, Before We Say "Goodnight," as what can and should be the experience of every child."

KEN CANFIELD, PH.D.,
Executive Director, Boone Center for the Family, Pepperdine University

"Hank Frazee's book confirms for us all that the best stories are the ones that are told from the heart...personal tales...family memories...that continue the tradition that began thousands of years ago around the campfire. It's a fantastic book!"

BEAU BRIDGES

"A parent's most important responsibility is teaching a child to know and worship his or her Creator. Hank Frazee shows how to incorporate our life experiences and moral values as an entertaining and instructive part of that responsibility and reveals how any parent can do it! Bravo!!"

PAT BOONE, Entertainer

"Children especially love two things: the first is stories, and the second is hearing about their parents' lives. Hank Frazee has wrapped both loves into one beautiful method and book. It should sweep the nation!"

DAN SULLIVAN, Founder of The Strategic Coach, Inc.

"You are a champion in the hearts and minds of your kids and they want to know all about you. This book is a knockout and will show you how to tell your story to your children."

GEORGE FOREMAN,
World Champion Heavyweight Boxer and Entrepreneur

"If we love reading and great stories, there is nothing better than passing these on to the next generation. Hank Frazee encourages us in creative ways to keep the important art of storytelling alive. A must for anyone with a story to tell."

JOHN WOOD,
Founder and Executive Chairman, *Room to Read*

"We love this book! Every parent (and grandparent) should read it. Before We Say "Goodnight" will revolutionize your tuck-in time with your children."

DRS. LES AND LESLIE PARROTT,
Founders of www.realrelationships.com, Authors of *The Parent You Want to Be*

"What a gift! Hank's book is more than "how to tell bedtime stories."
This book reveals the secret of strengthening the lifetime connection
between parents and children, while enhancing their brain development. The human voice and human touch are two of the most powerful
stimulators of the child's brain from birth onward, and parents who
sit with their children, or hold them while reading, are accomplish-
ing three purposes: building a close and meaningful relationship that
will last a lifetime, improving quality of brain activity, and sharing
cherished reflections of intimate bits of life history. Children who
experience story time with their parents will always reach for books,
and they will always want to learn to read. Preparing your children
for academic success is best achieved by reading and telling stories to
your children during their first three to four years of life. The more
personal the stories are the more memorable they will be for your
children. Hank's book sets the tone for you to enjoy a natural and
enlightening path to bonding with your children."

WANDA DRAPER, PH.D.,
Professor Emeritus, University of Oklahoma College of Medicine

"In this busy world, with increasingly pervasive modern technology,
this delightful book inspires us to share memories and stories with
our children. Hank Frazee has shown us how to instill family values
and traditions while enjoying the special time before our children
fall asleep. Though my children have grown, I will be thankful for
Hank's inspiration as I tell stories to my grandchildren."

DR. ANDREW MCLAREN, Pediatrician

"Before We Say "Goodnight" reminds us of the beauty of family, the
power of our stories, and the value of connection."

THEMA BRYANT-DAVIS, PH.D.
Author of *Thriving in the Wake of Trauma: A Multicultural Guide*

"Our children and grandchildren want to know who we really are. This book provides a wonderful method to share our life with those we love. It's out of this world!"

"Before We Say 'Goodnight' is absolutely wonderful and I loved it. I passed it on to another dear friend who has just had his grandchildren move within "goodnight story telling" distance. He too thought it was really helpful and VERY practical. Having to create stories is only for the gifted...like my dad, but for the rest of us mortals to be able to retell your own life story in little excerpts is wonderful and essential to keeping family history alive."

Before We Say "Goodnight"

How to Tell Bedtime Stories About Your Life and Family

Hank Frazee

NEW YORK

Before We Say "Goodnight"

How to Tell Bedtime Stories About Your Life and Family

Published in New York, New York, by Morgan James Publishing. Morgan James and The Entrepreneurial Publisher are trademarks of Morgan James, LLC.

www.MorganJamesPublishing.com

The Morgan James Speakers Group can bring authors to your live event. For more information or to book an event visit The Morgan James Speakers Group at

www.TheMorganJamesSpeakersGroup.com.

ISBN 978-1-61448-601-5 paperback
ISBN 978-1-61448-602-2 ebook
ISBN 978-1-61448-603-9 audio
ISBN 978-1-61448-891-0 hardcover
Library of Congress Control Number: 2010921782

Morgan James Publishing
The Entrepreneurial Publisher
5 Penn Plaza, 23rd Floor,
New York City, New York 10001
(212) 655-5470 office • (516) 908-4496 fax
www.MorganJamesPublishing.com

Cover Illustration by:
Brandon Jeffords
jeffordsart.blogspot.com

Interior Design by:
Peri Poloni-Gabriel
www.knockoutbooks.com

Edited by:
Elizabeth Frazee
Elizabeth@beforewesaygoodnight.com

FREE eBook edition for your existing eReader with purchase

PRINT NAME ABOVE

For more information, instructions, restrictions, and to download the BitLit app, go to **www.bitlit.ca** or use your QR Reader to scan:

In an effort to support local communities, raise awareness and funds, Morgan James Publishing donates a percentage of all book sales for the life of each book to Habitat for Humanity Peninsula and Greater Williamsburg.

Get involved today, visit
www.MorganJamesBuilds.com.

Habitat for Humanity
Peninsula and
Greater Williamsbur
Building Partner

Contents

To my wife, Liz,
for encouraging me always,
and to our children…
for listening.

—∞—

Foreword

Hank Frazee is an expert on the subject of how to tell a story, as he has told some 7,000 original bedtime stories about his life and family history to his three children over the last ten years. In *Before We Say "Goodnight,"* he shares the magic of storytelling and encourages us to join him on this life-changing journey with the children we love. The author entertains us with samples of his children's favorite stories and provides helpful suggestions and ideas for topics, how to tell a story and where to begin.

Busy as we all are, we may feel that we have neither the time nor the ability to tell our personal life stories in an interesting manner. With his engaging and ingenious writing style, Hank dispels these concerns and assists the reader to begin the storytelling experience by distilling the process into simple steps that are easy to follow.

Why is it that storytelling is so powerful? One reason might be that stories can be richer and more meaningful than photographs or a factual outline of one's life. Furthermore, it is through stories that we leave a legacy that outlives each of us. I personally want to leave such a legacy. And I know that if I follow Hank's example of storytelling, my own children, grandchildren and great grandchildren will really know me and, hopefully, they too will continue the tradition of storytelling in their own families.

You may embark on this adventure simply by telling a bedtime story when the opportunity initially presents itself. For many parents, this will become a nightly ritual. For others, it may be less often. But no matter the frequency, the children in your life will look forward to your special times together as you forge bonds that may last for generations to come. This practice sets the stage for the beliefs and values inherent in the stories of our lives to emerge and inspire young minds with invaluable lessons.

I have spent my life as an educator, author, and co-founder of an online storybooking company, Heritage Makers, with the objective of assisting individuals to publish the stories of their lives. Stories are rarely forgotten, and when they are written and bound into books, they're among our most treasured possessions.

One can never underestimate the power and legacy that family stories can establish. And who can tell how one's influence will be felt in the generations to come. I encourage you to read *Before We Say "Goodnight,"* itself a deeply rewarding experience, and begin the journey of a lifetime with the children you love.

Sharon Gibb Murdoch, Ed.D.
Co-founder, Heritage Makers
www.storybookingheritage.com

"Write what you know about."

MARK TWAIN

—〰—

Introduction

We live in challenging times. Our daily lives as parents can be complex, demanding and sometimes wildly busy. Allow me to make three assumptions we likely share. We love our kids, we have a story to tell and we want to pass it on to them. Passing wisdom and experience from generation to generation is at the very heart of good storytelling as well as parenting. If you want to deepen your relationship with your kids and are willing to invest a few minutes a day in doing so, you've come to the right place.

I know how to tell bedtime stories and have been doing so nightly with my three kids for over a decade. This book will show you how and why to tell the stories of your life and family to your children or grandchildren. Each chapter shares insights and techniques that I have developed in my own storytelling and is followed by stories that I have told to my children. Telling stories will bring you closer to your kids and open up your communication with them as they grow older. And if you're like me, that's something you want. Take a look at the first chapter and you'll get a good idea of where we're headed.

Before We Say "Goodnight" will show you how to tell great bedtime stories to your children, which they will never forget. I'm not talking about *reading* them a story, though that's a good idea. I'm talking about *telling* them the stories of your life and family, one night at a time. Intimidating, impossible, boring, you say? Well, it is possible, a lot of fun and you can do it. As you'll see throughout the book, there are numerous benefits to doing so. You'll improve their vocabulary, listening and comprehension skills, for instance, and you'll do it without even trying. But don't feel that you have to tell a story every night. That's entirely up to you.

In this book, you'll discover an easy-to-learn three-step method to turn your life experiences, and those of your family, into great bedtime stories. You'll also discover the many reasons why telling bedtime stories can be a terrific part of your life with your children. Rest assured, this book is *not* about telling one long and endlessly dull story of your family history. It's about how to tell new and entertaining stories each night, in any order you want, about your life and family experiences.

You'll also learn why you'll never run out of stories to tell, using Story Prompting, a technique I invented for my own storytelling. This method requires no notes or preparation and is easy to learn.

Once you've read *Before We Say "Goodnight,"* it can be used as a helpful reference or shared with family and friends, for their own storytelling adventures. Tell your stories. Your kids want to hear them.

Hank Frazee

1

The Beginning

"Two roads diverged in a wood, and I—
I took the one less traveled by,
and that has made all the difference."

ROBERT FROST

I **have told over seven thousand** bedtime stories to my three children and rarely repeated any of them. Yes, I've done the math. I tell my kids an original story every night, before they go to sleep. And they ask for one every night. What's more important is that you can do it too. You don't have to be well-read, and you don't need a great memory or speaking voice. You just need to be *you* and follow a few simple guidelines. This book will show you how it's done.

You'll learn a lot by reading the stories that follow each chapter. They all follow my basic formula for storytelling, as outlined in this book, and will be easy for you to duplicate with your own children. These are stories that my kids particularly enjoyed, and they will give you a good idea of how to tell a story. I always adjust the story to the audience, based on their age and maturity. The stories are presented here just as I've told them to my kids, with a few exceptions. I've titled them for the book, included occasional italicized or parenthetical remarks and made some minor changes for clarity and emphasis. I've also left out the questions and answers that often follow a story.

You have the ability to tell your kids great bedtime stories that they will always remember. All it really takes is your life experience and the desire to connect with your children. You have a built-in advantage in that you have a captive audience, your kids.

Think about it. It's bedtime. Your kids and you are worn out, but they want to wring one more ounce of fun out of the day before they go to sleep. They want a bedtime story, and they are ready to really *listen* to *your* story. Unless you have an incredible memory and can draw up great stories at the end of a typically exhausting day and then tell them well, night after night, you won't make it with fairy tales. Thankfully, you have a vast and virtually endless supply of stories from your life experience. There are several advantages to this fact:

- You don't have to prepare anything in advance
- Your kids are interested in who you are and were before they were born
- Your stories are naturally infused with your values
- You are sharing the oral history of their family
- You don't have to tell your stories in any particular order
- You'll never run out of material
- Telling bedtime stories can create a tradition of storytelling in your family which can last for generations.

In reality, these stories could be told anytime. Yet at night, when kids are sleepy and the lights are out, they are perhaps more willing to let Mom or Dad just talk. For the sake of simplicity, when I use the words "parent," "mom" or "dad" in this book, I'm referring to anyone who is important in the life of a child. And everyone has a story to tell. If there is more than one adult in your family, you can trade off telling stories, and don't feel pressured that you have to tell a story every night. You'll find the pace that's right for you.

But what if you're not the one who puts them to bed? No problem. You can tell your stories anytime and anywhere, at a family dinner or vacation, driving to school or even on the phone or through email. If you are a grandparent, your family may have suggested interviewing you to capture the family history. Why not beat them to the punch by *telling* your story now? The guidelines in this book will show you how, and they apply just as well to stories away from bedtime as those told before we say, "Goodnight."

One more comment about timing: the intent of bedtime stories is to entertain and connect with our children. Occasionally, my kids will find a story frightening or upsetting. I was surprised that what

I thought was a funny story about getting my tonsils out had that effect on them. On the rare occasion this happens, I change to another story. I am trying to soothe them to sleep, not keep them awake with worries. There are of course other family stories that are better told to more mature children, when they are ready, away from bedtime.

I always tell bedtime stories with the lights out, because there are fewer distractions to the story and the kids keep heading in the direction of sleep. And my memories are easier to access in the dark. When I told my brother-in-law Bill that I was writing this book, he told me the following story:

"When I was a kid in Pittsburgh, my grandfather would sometimes put us to bed and tell us stories. The lights were always out, and he was usually smoking his pipe. He told us about his life and adventures. In the dark, there were just

6

the sound of his voice and the glow of
the pipe, and, when he would take a puff, I
could see his face."

I love that story because it's about Bill's love
for his grandfather and vice versa, and it's a
memory he will always treasure. Bedtime stories
are a pathway to a great inheritance—your love
for your children and the stories of their family.
Don't miss it.

*Note to the reader: The stories that follow each
chapter are told just as I told them to my children.
I refer to Grandpa, Grammy and Aunt Mary Ellen.
This is how my children think of them, while in fact
they are my parents and my sister. I refer to others
as Aunts or Uncles, while they may be aunts, uncles,
cousins or other close friends.*

A Hot Breakfast

One of my earliest memories happened
at breakfast when I was about two and a half.
Grandpa was out of town on a business trip, and
Aunt Mary Ellen and I were having our breakfast
with Grammy. I was sitting in my high chair, as
usual, at the kitchen table.

You know how Grammy and Grandpa like
antiques? Well, we had a round oak table in
the kitchen, where we ate breakfast and most all
of our meals. It was covered with a tablecloth,
designed with brightly colored flowers. Aunt
Mary Ellen must have been about five. It was a
school day, and Grammy was hurrying to get
us fed, in order to get Aunt Mary Ellen off to
kindergarten.

Grammy put a piece of bread in the toaster
which sat on the other side of the table. Then
she heard the trash truck coming down the

street. Grandpa had asked her to be sure to put the trash cans out the night before, and she had forgotten. She jumped up, telling Aunt Mary Ellen to watch me and ran outside to take the trash cans to the street before the workers got there. Well, the moment she went out one door, Aunt Mary Ellen, being an active kid, went out the other.

And I sat there alone eating my oatmeal; that is, until something strange began to happen. Smoke started to come out of the toaster. At first, it was just a little wisp, but it caught my attention. It went straight up like one of those ropes in the cartoons that comes out of a snake charmer's basket.

As I watched it, the smoke grew darker and wider. Pretty soon, smoke was coming out from under the toaster too. And that's when the table caught on fire.

Luckily, I wasn't that close to it, so I just kept

watching it to see what would happen next. Suddenly I heard a terrible scream which scared the heck out of me, as Grammy came running into the room and grabbed me out of my high chair. She unplugged the toaster from the wall, ran to the cupboard and grabbed a big pitcher. She filled it with water and threw the water on the fire, as horrible hissing sounds and a great plume of white smoke filled the room.

I didn't get my piece of toast that morning. And for quite a while after that, if you looked under the tablecloth, which I did often, you could see a big black spot where the toaster had been.

━━━ ━━ ━

2

The Best Storyteller
On The Planet

"Nothing you do for a child is ever wasted."

GARRISON KEILLOR

—⚬—

Who is the best storyteller on the planet? As far as your kids are concerned, you are, because the story you have to tell is the story of *your* life, and only you can tell it from your unique perspective. That's the story your kids want to hear because they love you. And the way to show them that you love them is by spending your time with them, particularly in the evening as they drift off to sleep.

Children love to spend time with you that is focused on you and them together. But there is too much to do and too much going on, almost all the time. Often I am so rushed, with trying to get everything done, that I try to fool myself and my kids into thinking that running eight errands on a Saturday, with them tagging along, is the same as spending time with them hanging out or playing catch or ping pong. It's not. Bedtime stories are a great way to spend some time together, away from the rush of daily life.

This brings us to the topic of this book: you and your story and why this method works so well. You can tell your story better than anyone, because you've lived it. You don't need any notes. You don't need to plan it in advance, and you can rattle it off as easy as can be. And that is exactly what I'll show you how to do.

Let's start with some basics to get you going. We'll add detail and technique as you read through the book, building on your experience. In Chapters 10 and 11, we'll go through the whole method start to finish. By the end of the book, you'll know exactly how to tell a bedtime story every night, if you wish, with little or no preparation.

You might ask, where do you begin in telling a story? Start with a person, or animal, or both. These people or animals will be the main characters of your story. They need to be doing something, either by themselves or with someone else. The story develops from telling the listener about the action or experience that your characters are engaged in. Put that action or experience in a logical order with a beginning, middle and an end. Add a few details and you will have a story. Remember, a story is not simply a recitation of facts. A story tells of a specific person, or animal, engaged in a specific action or experience.

Let me give you a brief example. "My dad grew up in Lawrence, Kansas." If I simply continue relating his personal statistics, this will be a recitation of facts, not a story. However, if I choose a specific experience he had, I immediately step into story mode. Add a beginning, middle and end, and a story begins to emerge. The more specific and detailed the experience, the better. Think of it as painting a picture with words.

To begin again, "When my dad was a kid, growing up in Lawrence, Kansas, he and his friends were really into animals, wild and otherwise. Somehow, he got a baby alligator and decided to keep it as a pet. He figured an alligator needed to be near water, so he put it in the laundry tub in the basement of his parent's house. Oh, and he somehow forgot to tell his mother that he had an alligator or where he was keeping it. So when she went down into the dark basement to do the laundry and found an alligator in the tub, you can imagine how loudly she screamed because of the alligator and then at him. That was the end of having an alligator as a pet, though not the end of your grandpa's love of animals, wild and otherwise."

Let's review. The story above involves characters, my dad and his mother and a baby alligator, taking action or having a specific experience. Though brief, this story has a beginning, my dad finding the alligator; the middle, putting the alligator in the basement tub; and the end, my grandmother's sudden discovery and the immediate departure of the alligator. Adding detail fills in the picture. You'll find that each of the stories in this book follows this structural pattern. Watch for this pattern, model it and you'll be on your way to telling your own great bedtime stories.

Grandpa and the Pig

When Aunt Mary Ellen got her first house, it was in a part of town where all of the properties were set up like little farms. She had a small house toward the front of a large rectangular lot, with a typical backyard. And behind that yard was a farm.

She had a long barn on one side of the remaining lot that reached most of the way to the back of the property, for farm animals, such as horses, goats and chickens. On the other side of the yard was a garden to grow food such as corn, lettuce and tomatoes, really vegetables of every kind. There was a small orchard of fruit trees with apples, oranges and lemons. When you think about it, almost all the food you would need could be grown or raised right there on her little farm. Behind the barn, a corral covered the width of the remaining lot and was used as a turnout for the barnyard animals.

Grandpa used to love to go over there, I think because it reminded him of his childhood. He grew up in a small town in Kansas. In those days, the town was surrounded by farms, and you can bet there were plenty of farms within a few minutes of his house. Most everyone had a vegetable garden to grow at least part of their own food, and a lot of people kept chickens for eggs too. Grandpa's favorite thing to do in Aunt Mary Ellen's yard was to rake leaves. I think he found it relaxing after a hard week's work.

Now then, Aunt Mary Ellen's neighbor had a pig, a very large pig, a Yorkshire, which had white pointy ears. He probably weighed close to a thousand pounds, was about six feet long and nearly three feet tall. The pig liked to roll in the mud to stay cool on a hot day. A five-foot tall wooden fence ran the length of the property, separating Aunt Mary Ellen's and her neighbor's yards. The pig lived in a small mud-covered pen just on the other side of the fence.

Anyway, one warm afternoon Grandpa was out in back, raking up leaves under a huge walnut tree. And there were a lot of leaves because it was fall. He stopped to rest and went over to the fence to take a look at the pig, as it was snorting around in its pen. Grandpa was probably daydreaming about *his* grandfather's farm and stood there quietly for several moments, admiring the pig.

After a while, Grandpa gently said, "Hey Pig," and that's when the trouble began. Because the fence was high, the pig hadn't seen or heard Grandpa walk up. The pig was startled by the sound of Grandpa's voice and, in panic, whipped its head around to see where this sudden threat was coming from. Only Grandpa's face was showing over the fence, and, as the pig spun its head around, along with it came all of the slop from its snout. The pig slop went flying through the air, with the greatest of ease, and hit Grandpa square in the face.

Well, you can imagine Grandpa was fairly startled himself and pretty grossed out too, standing there with a rake in one hand and pig slop all over his face. But after he cleaned up, he thought it was pretty funny and enjoyed telling that story to the family.

From then on, however, Grandpa made sure to let the pig know he was there, before he went over to have a look.

3

A Boy and His Dad

"Do the best you can and don't take life too serious."

WILL ROGERS

—∿—

My wife and I are both big readers. We love to read, and all of the employees at our favorite bookstore turn and smile whenever we walk in. When we had our first child, John, we resolved that he would be a reader too. We decided that the best way to make that happen was to read to him every night, when we put him to bed. Clever, huh? Sometimes Liz would read, sometimes both of us would read, and we rarely missed a night.

Over time, we fell into a routine that Liz would read to him, then turn out the lights and sit with him for a few minutes. Then I would come in and sit for a while, until he got sleepy. He had us fairly well-trained. Russell Baker sums it up nicely, "When you're the only pea in the pod, your parents may sometimes have trouble distinguishing you from the Hope Diamond."

As John got older and this routine became well-ingrained, he began to ask me for a bedtime story. I began with "Goldilocks" and then "The Three Little Pigs," "Little Red Riding Hood" and "Jack and the Beanstalk." After that, I was pretty much out of material. Though I had majored in English literature in college, I couldn't think of any other stories to tell or condense in a way that would have any real meaning, or be entertaining, to a two-year-old. So I did what any of you would do. I went back to "Goldilocks" and changed the script. John found this mildly entertaining for a few days, but that was about it.

Then I switched to nonsensical stories made up on the spur of the moment with no real plot or point, which are harder to pull off after a full day of work and kids. You may be one of those parents who have the gift to make up a great story out of thin air that is entertaining to both you and your kids. However, if you're like me, telling this kind of story at the end of a long day, on an empty tank of gas, just leaves my kids saying, "Huh?" When I've attempted to pass off one of these dogs onto my kids, they start barking.

So, having run through my short list of fairy tales and nonsense stories, I had no bedtime stories left to tell. Then, out of the blue, I thought to ask John if he wanted a "real" bedtime story or a "fake" one. He of course had no idea of what I was talking about. I began to explain the difference between the two, making it up as I went along. I said, "A 'fake' story didn't really happen, but a 'real' story did." He looked at me for a second and said, "I want a 'real' story about something that really happened."

What I had in mind was to tell him something that I had done as a kid, which he would find interesting and could relate to. Suddenly, I realized there were countless experiences to choose from. From that night on, as I came into the room and he asked for a bedtime story, I replied, "Real or fake?" And he would *always* say, "Real!" Bless him.

I was off the hook then and there. And so are you. You have a lifetime of your own experiences, and your family's experiences, to share with your children. You're the only one who can tell them your "real" story, and, believe me, they want to hear it. The best way I've found to remember my experiences is by using Story Prompters, explained in detail in Chapter 10, which is a cross-referencing system to jog your memory. Use it and you will never run out of stories to tell.

The wonderful thing is that you don't have to tell your story in chronological order. In fact, it's better if you don't. I just tell the story that occurs to me that night, and over time the picture of our life and family emerges. My kids make the connections themselves, and each story stands on its own. Further, using this method, the stories are less likely to come off as one long lecture, which is much easier on you and your kids. As you read along, start telling your own stories following the guidelines in the book. Your stories will improve as you practice. And soon, you will be telling them with ease.

Note to the reader: As background to the following story, my Aunt Janice and Uncle Gordon had a log cabin above Lake Tahoe, where I spent some of the best days of my childhood. Each summer, our family and many of our friends made the sojourn "up to the cabin" during the last days of August. The property was owned by a group of families, but my aunt and uncle and their kids were the only ones who actually lived there year-round. Most of the other families came up just for a day of fishing on the small lake. Some stayed a weekend or so in the only guest house on the property. The land was otherwise undeveloped, except for a caretaker's cabin and a small boathouse. Surrounded on three sides by national forest, the cabin and everything about it was heaven on earth to me.

As we turned off the highway onto the unmarked dirt road, the fragrance of pine trees and dust filled our noses and senses. Our excitement grew, as we rolled up the windows for the ride down the winding road. The cabin lay before us, getting closer by the moment, while a cloud of dust and memories of daily life at home drifted behind.

I can still hear the sound of the Swiss cowbell out front, being rung to call all us kids to lunch: peanut butter and jelly sandwiches on a paper towel, with one Oreo cookie and a small Dixie cup filled with ice-cold milk. We hand-cranked homemade ice cream out on the front steps, after barbeques on the patio with my parents, aunts and uncles and all of my cousins, in an eternal summer that seemed as though it would never end.

Snakes and Bumblebees

When we were up at the cabin as kids, we spent a lot of time building forts, going on hikes to hunt for arrowheads, tramping back and forth to the lake to go fishing or rowing and anything else we could find to have fun. We played in the stream, skipped rocks, and went on picnics, roasting hot dogs and marshmallows on hand-cut willow sticks. And there were always plenty of kids around to play with, my cousins, of course, and whoever else might be visiting.

One of our favorite activities was to go snake hunting, though we could do it only when there was no wind. Usually, just the boys went hunting. We had a blast, but it took a little courage too.

We walked down to the far side of the lake, close to where the stream came in. We tried to be very quiet at this point, as we peered through the trees to catch a glimpse of the grass along this remote part of the shoreline. If there was no breeze, which was fairly uncommon because there is almost always a breeze high up in the mountains, we knew we had a chance to catch a snake. When the wind is still, the grass is still also, and you can easily see the movement of any creature in it. We crept to the edge of the grass, which was about a foot or two high and twenty feet wide along the shoreline. We spread out and stomped loudly through the grass. Before us, the grass was completely still, unless there was something hiding in it that began to rush away from us as we got closer.

If the grass moved quickly and in a straight line, we knew there was likely a mouse scurrying away. But if it moved more slowly in a waving motion, we hoped to catch a snake! We raced toward it and dove our hands into the grass, not *really* sure what might be there. We grabbed at whatever we touched. And when we pulled up our hands, we often had a wriggling snake.

The snake was as excited as we were, though for different reasons. But after a while everyone settled down, and the snake curled around our hands and arms. They were all garter snakes and, when threatened, released a foul odor. They would stink, as did we, so everyone was happy.

If we caught a small snake, we would put it in our shirt pocket and run back up to the cabin to show everyone. We'd ask our mothers to take a look in our pockets and scare the heck out of them. If the snake was a larger one, we'd bring it out from behind our backs and scare the heck out of them. A great time was had by all, well, most of us--well, at least us boys.

Other times, we'd go out hunting for Chinese bumblebees. "Hunting" is probably the wrong word since they were pretty much everywhere. Chinese bumblebees are smaller and two-tone yellow and black, rather than the all black of your basic model. At such a high elevation, the little yellow flowering plants that attracted the bees were quite scrubby and dusty and close to the ground, and, come to think of it, so were we. Now the crucial tool to have with you when you go hunting for Chinese bumblebees is an empty Heinz pickle jar. They were made of glass with a green metal screw-on lid and still are.

We'd have a contest to see who could catch the most Chinese bumblebees in one jar, at the same time, without getting stung. And our hunting technique was always the same. We'd squat down next to a plant where a bee was buzzing, open the lid just a crack, clamp it quickly over the bee and drag it back. Voila! The hunt was on.

The first one was easy but the next ones became more and more challenging. With each additional bee we'd go after, the chances of one or more escaping and stinging us became greater, though we were pretty darned good at it and could easily get over a dozen bees in the jar without too much trouble. When we got up to around twenty, the odds started to work against us. The bees were getting madder and more crowded by the moment, and the danger of getting stung increased with each new capture. I think twenty-five was about the upper limit.

We had a great time looking at the bees in the jar, from behind the glass barrier. But after a while, we grew bored and too afraid to try for more. We began to feel sorry for the bees and wondered how to get them out of the jar without getting stung. Throwing the jar occurred to us but we never did that. We didn't want to hurt the bees, and we didn't want them to hurt us either. The best method, in fact the only method we used, was to place the jar on the ground and get in a good sideways squatting position. We'd rip the lid off as quickly as possible, while springing away and running like mad. That was always exciting and a great way to entertain ourselves, on a summer day up at the cabin.

━━ ━━ ━━

4

Time Travelers

*"The best and most beautiful things in the
world cannot be seen or even touched.
They must be felt with the heart."*

HELEN KELLER

—〰—

Six years after our son was born, our twin
girls arrived. Surprise! We were hoping for
another child and were blessed with two beautiful daughters. Naturally, I wanted to tell them
bedtime stories too, and I did, early on. I think
children learn quickly just from hearing us speak,
and have noticed that they find the sound of our

voice soothing and comforting as they drift off to sleep.

Our daughters love the stories, and we look forward to them together. I never know what I'm going to say, and I kind of like that. The stories I tell are a surprise to all of us. Yet they do fill out the picture of who I am and was as a child, and I enjoy reliving those memories with them. If I begin telling a story they've already heard, they say, "You told us this one." I usually challenge them with, "Okay, then tell me how it goes." And they will, in amazing detail. They're listening and they remember the stories of their family.

I've always loved the idea of time travel. *Back to the Future* is one of my favorite movies. How incredible it would be to travel through time and see Lincoln at Gettysburg, our country in 1776, my father as a boy. Every night I go time-traveling with my children, and you can too with your children. The best time machine ever invented is sitting right there on your shoulders.

My mother knows more of our history than anyone in the family and has shared it with me throughout my life. I am passing that story on to my children because it's fun and gives us a deeper sense of identity, purpose and meaning. My kids know the names and stories of most of our family. They also know that the big oak rocking chair in our den has been used by every generation of our family back to Sarah Maxfield, their great-great-great-grandmother who was also the mother of twins.

Grandpa Hawley, her son-in-law, owned that rocking chair, and I know more about him than any of my other great-grandparents. He was the sheriff of a small town and then moved to Seattle in the early 1900s to go into the rock and gravel business. Grandpa Hawley, as we all call him, was instrumental in the construction of downtown Seattle and the early landmark buildings of Los Angeles. He led a remarkable life and went broke three times along the way. He finished on top, was devoted to his family and had a good sense of humor. How do I know so much about him? It's because he wrote and self-published his autobiography, and everyone in the family has a copy. You could do that. Anyone can, because everyone has a story to tell.

Grandpa Hawley was a pioneer "time traveler" in our family, and his book had a big impact on me. Whether we write a book or tell stories, we touch our kids in all that we do with them. We also touch the future generations of our families, whom we will never meet. Let me prove it to you with the following questions:

- Did your parents influence you?

- Did their parents influence them?

- Did the influence their parents had on them have an influence on you?

- Will you have an influence on your children?

The answer to all these questions is, of course, yes. The experience of all those who went before us influences us, as we influence those who follow us. How we use language, view our world and everything in between, are influenced by ancestors we've never met.

I travel back in time when I tell a bedtime story. And that story and how I am with my children travel forward in time with them. If you have no plans to start writing your life story, how about telling it instead? The average story takes less than five minutes to tell. How much more sense of self, family and belonging will our children have with a tradition of storytelling like this? Your family's tradition of oral history can begin with you.

Our daughter said to me the other night at story time, "You sure have had a lot of adventures, Dad!" And so have you and your family, and you can tell those adventures to your children one by one, night by night, just as I am doing. Remember this, be it ever so humble, there's no story like your own.

If you would like a simple technique to interview your parents or grandparents, please visit us at beforewesaygoodnight.com/interview.

Winston

When I was a kid, I lived at Grammy and Grandpa's house, as you know. After I graduated from college, I began my business and shared a house with Aunt Mary Ellen for a while. When I saved up enough money, I bought a small house where I lived on my own. This was, of course, before Mom and I met and got married. I was at work all day and sometimes in the evening too. On the weekends, I might be home but was often out with friends or sometimes away on business or vacation.

In any case, that didn't leave much room for a pet, and what I wanted most was a dog. I've always been a dog man and thought it would be great to have a dog to play with and to keep me company. On the other hand, wouldn't it be unfair for the dog to stay home all day by himself? And what about when I was out of town? He'd have to go to a lonely old kennel, so I didn't get a dog. I figured that I'd wait until I got married and had kids. And that was that— until I met Winston or, actually, his brother.

One day, I was in a local store, and there sitting in a corner was an English bulldog. Now, I had never really wanted a bulldog, all that snorting and slobbering, kind of short and slow. And this dog was really slow, he didn't move at all. I always figured I'd get a yellow or black lab, more of a sporting dog. Even so, this bulldog was really beautiful, in an ugly sort of way. He was brown and white with some black spots and big black eyes. He had a dignified way, and as he sat there, quite regally, I thought this could be the dog for me. If I was out all day or away on a trip, I sensed he wouldn't mind. The trouble was, he wasn't for sale.

He did, however, have a brother and I arranged to buy him that day. The people I bought him from gave me a container to take him home in, and I stopped at the pet store to get him a bowl. When I got home, I realized that I had forgotten to buy him a collar. Just then, I remembered my grandmother's German shepherd named Dirk. He was a great dog, and all of us cousins loved him, and he loved us and was very protective of us too. When he died, my grandmother had given me his collar, and I had saved it all these years. I went to get it out of the drawer I'd kept it in, and it fit my new dog perfectly.

Even though the collar said "Dirk," I decided to name my dog after Winston Churchill, the Prime Minister of England during World War II. Mr. Churchill was one of the most important men in history, and his nickname was "The Bull Dog." Grandpa's dad, my grandfather, met him on several occasions, but I'll tell you that story another time. Anyway, the name "Winston" seemed to suit my dog well. He was strong and looked wise and tough, too. He was always near the front door with his collar on and his dog bowl in front of him.

Did I mention that Winston was made of plaster of paris? As a matter of fact, he was. But he was life-sized and painted brindle and white, and, whenever anyone would come in, they did a quick double-take when they saw him. He looked *completely* real and was quite popular with my friends. They all greeted him by name. I think he liked that.

He didn't mind if I was out all day or even for a week. I don't think he missed me at all, and he never went to the bathroom in the house. In fact, he never went anywhere. He'd simply sit there looking at the front door. That dog won any staring contest paws down, and he even knew a few tricks. He could sit, stay or play dead and was very well mannered.

The best part about having Winston was when my friends brought *their* dogs over. The same thing happened every time. The visiting dog happily trotted into the house ready to sniff everything in sight, but froze and stared the moment it saw Winston. Winston stared back. This really upset the visiting dog, and its hackles went up. Then, slowly, the visitor would realize that Winston wasn't real. And at that moment, the real dog would blush and get a look on its face as if to say, "I knew all along that dog wasn't real." *Sure you did.*

But if you were watching very closely just then, and it may have been my imagination, as it was fairly subtle, Winston would smile.

——— —— —

5

Purpose and Meaning

"You know the only people who are always
sure about the proper way to raise children?
Those who've never had any."

BILL COSBY

As a kid, I preferred playing outside or hanging out with my friends over studying and doing homework. As an adult, however, I am highly goal-oriented and have been since I began college. That quality helped me become successful in business. Yet, I believe that being too purposeful can get in the way of good parenting. There's a fine line that every parent walks between being purposeful and just being with our children.

I've not abandoned my goals for myself or our children. Even so, I try to make time each day simply to be with them, where there is no goal in mind other than to enjoy one another's company. When I do that, we all enjoy the rest of the day more as well. This non-instructive time can last for a few minutes, such as admiring an art project they have done for school, to an hour or more depending on what we're doing. We may play ping pong, four-square or a board game together. Sometimes we're just sitting on the couch reading or watching a movie. The emphasis in all these times is on being together.

So how does that apply to telling bedtime stories? It is that I don't have any agenda when I tell a story. It's not about the story, it's about being together. Generally, I don't make any notes or plan the story in advance. I don't think about it at all until the moment I tell it. At that point, I just tell whatever story comes to mind. If I can't think of a story, I use Story Prompters, my memory jogging system to help me get going.

In our house, the routine has become for us to say prayers together. Then Liz reads to the girls, and our son finishes up his homework. When Liz has finished reading, I come in and tell them a story. We spend much of our day, as parents, in the instructive mode. That's not what story time is about. We are not overtly teaching anything here. Yet among the many benefits of telling bedtime stories is that we *indirectly* teach our children the life lessons and values inherent in any good story.

Remember, a story is not a lecture, it's a story. It's fine for them to ask questions for clarification.

Be spontaneous and interactive. Rude interruptions, however, are not allowed. Luckily, there is a surefire way to limit interruptions. I calmly say, "Please stop interrupting, or I will stop telling the story," and they stop. Remember that line, you'll need it. Don't get into an argument or start yelling at them. There is plenty of opportunity for that at other times during the day. My idea is to spend meaningful time with my kids, and for us to go to bed happy and secure in our relationship.

One of the best storytellers I ever knew was my mom's cousin Harold McMurrin. Harold had been a singer and actor on Broadway in his youth. He had a rich baritone and great delivery, what I came to think of as the McMurrin voice. Harold loved to tell stories, and everyone loved to hear him tell them. He would lean forward, one arm draped over his knee and a twinkle in his eye. He was as interested in the story as we were—a guaranteed recipe for a good story.

Harold was a real character. He was funny and loved to laugh with you, at you and at himself. He could say outrageous things that would get you in trouble in most families. All the same, Harold could get away with it. Harold and Sandy were married for thirty plus years, and she enjoyed his sense of humor as much as anyone. I remember Harold announcing, with Sandy present, "Today is my fiftieth wedding anniversary." Everyone knew they hadn't been married that long. Harold patiently explained that this was indeed his fiftieth wedding anniversary—if you went back to his first marriage and counted all four of his marriages together. He had a way of saying things that made Sandy and everyone else laugh.

Harold was the youngest of four brothers, all of whom passed away before him. When Harold announced that he was the last of the Mc Murrins, his nephew Bill said, "That's not true. I'm a McMurrin, and what about your three kids, not to mention all your other McMurrin relatives?" Harold wouldn't budge, "No, I'm the last of the McMurrins," he insisted.

"How do you figure that?" asked Bill, incredulously. "Because your mothers have diluted the gene pool," replied Harold, unmoved. My mother is a McMurrin too and really laughed when she heard that one. Harold had a special talent for commentary.

I used to study him when he spoke, wondering what it was about Harold that made his storytelling so entertaining. Maybe it was his actor's training, but I think it was his mischievous enjoyment of life that made him fascinating. You see, he had a conspiratorial way of telling a story, as though only a select few would ever hear his tale. "You see," was one of his signature phrases and always drew me in.

So, why am I telling you about Harold? For one, it's to suggest that you use his methods to make your stories more interesting to your children. Voice, tone, inflection, body posture and a twinkle in your eye will engage your audience and draw you closer...you see? When Harold went into the hospital in his final days, just shy of ninety, he was in a weakened condition. The doctors, testing his alertness, asked him if he knew who the President was. Harold admitted that he didn't, and after a moment added, "But I'm sure it's the wrong guy."

Here's my point. It's *purposeful* for me to clean out the garage, and that needs to be done. But it's *meaningful* to play a game with my family, hang out with my kids or tell them a bedtime story. Which will make more difference to them and to me in the long run? Harold was telling stories, sharing the family history and making people laugh until nearly ninety. That's possible for all of us. We tell a story in everything we do, and the people that story has the most influence on are our children. What kind of influence is up to us, and that's a choice we can make every day and night.

A Love of Horses

Aunt Janice had horses in her blood. At five, she pounded six nails into a small stick to make a horse, one nail for the head, four for the legs and, of course, one for the tail. At ten, she advanced to bigger ideas, using a long board for the body, a smaller one for the head and some string for the reins. Then she made herself a herd. Using a card table as her barn, she opened a riding stable at the curb in front of her house. Her sign boldly advertised, "Hobby Horses for Rent." I doubt she made much money, but she had fun and loved her horses.

When she was thirteen, she got a job at a real stable in Los Angeles, which kept several dozen ponies for children's parties and weekend rides. The Pony Park was still the site of many birthday parties when I was a kid. She worked there for free for the first year or so, mucking corrals, cleaning the barn and walking little kids around on the ponies, anything to be near horses. Aunt Janice was also a good artist, and what do you think she liked to draw and paint the most? You're right, horses. She had a dream of one day having her own horse farm. And do you know what? You can do anything you want if you keep working at it. And she did.

Every summer, she would go to her Aunt Cora and Uncle Ralph's ranch with her sister and her parents. She always hoped there would be a pony there for her, but there never was. Even so, she kept dreaming. Aunt Janice worked at the pony track until she was sixteen, gradually earning up to fifty cents an hour, all the while falling more and more in love with horses. You know you love horses if you like the smell of horse manure. I guess I have horses in my blood too, because that smell always makes me feel good.

Later in high school, Aunt Janice and her soon-to-become sister-in-law, Aunt Patsy, bought a matched pair of painted ponies and kept them at Griffith Park, where they could ride in the ring or on the trails nearby. She married Uncle Dale when she was twenty and moved to Georgia, when he went into the Army. She bought another horse named Sailor in Georgia. My cousins, your Aunt Lynne and Uncle Stephen, were born there.

Soon after they returned from Georgia, Uncle Dale passed away. They lived across the street from us, and we were all very sad when that happened. I felt particularly bad for my cousins who lost their father. He was a good uncle and always nice to me. When I was little, I had about twenty-five pictures of Navy ships, kept together by a rubber band. I told Uncle Dale that my daddy had been on every one of those ships during the war, and he was kind enough to believe me.

When Aunt Janice met Uncle Gordon and got married, they moved to his house that had a barn and room for horses. She taught all of us cousins to ride in her corral. She knew how to treat horses and if you didn't do it right, she'd let you have it. I remember she always seemed to have four to six horses there and a couple of ponies. Ponies can be mean, and I'll tell you another story tomorrow about one named Twinkle that was really mean.

Aunt Janice and Uncle Gordon eventually moved up to the cabin at Lake Tahoe with most of their kids and all of their horses. I have great memories of riding through the forest up there on horseback. If you ask me, there's no place more peaceful than riding a trail on the back of a horse.

All the while living up at the cabin, Aunt Janice kept thinking about that horse farm. She hadn't forgotten her dream, and she would talk about it from time to time. She began to look around for land to build it on and finally settled on forty acres between Reno and Carson City. They bought the land and built a first-class equestrian center, which now has over one hundred horses boarded there. Eventually, Franktown Meadows became one of the finest equestrian centers in the whole country.

And to think, it all started with a little girl who had a couple of sticks, a handful of nails *and a dream.*

6

Challenges of Fatherhood

"The most important thing you or I will ever do is within the walls of our own homes."

HAROLD B. LEE

—〰—

Sometimes daily life gets in the way of good storytelling and good parenting. I've noticed that the more relaxed and centered I am, the better my parenting and storytelling becomes. That's not to say that you have to feel blissfully happy and relaxed to tell a good bedtime story. If I waited for that, I'd probably never tell one. Thankfully, the very act of telling a bedtime story is centering and makes me more at ease. My guess is that you might experience this too. So I'd like to share some of the strategies I use to be a better parent and storyteller.

My aim as a father is to instill faith in my children, love of family and friends, enjoyment of life and work and a sincere desire to help others. I like the ideals characterized by Atticus Finch and Andy of Mayberry. Atticus is the small-town lawyer and father of Scout, the narrator in Harper Lee's Pulitzer Prize winning book, *To Kill a Mocking Bird*. The character of Atticus was based on Harper Lee's own father. Gregory Peck played Atticus in the movie. Firm but fair, wise and loving with his children, he fits my image of the character exactly. He is the embodiment of his moral values and stands up for what he believes in, alone if necessary. Andy of Mayberry, from the show of the same name, is kind and good-humored. Plain and simple, these guys are men. Children need men, and they especially need their fathers.

Though I aim for a combination of Atticus and Andy with my kids, kind, good-humored and wise, I rarely succeed for a whole day and at times not even for a few minutes. Sometimes, instead of Atticus and Andy I end up more like Dr. Jekyll and Mr. Hyde. But children need a mentor more than they need a critic, and I try to keep that in mind when my patience is wearing thin. At story time, I want my kids to feel comforted by my love for them before we say goodnight. That's really why I tell bedtime stories. And I suppose this book evolved out of my wish to share what I've learned with you.

Personally, I find endless challenge in work, marriage, parenting and life, in general. Lee

Iacocca said, "We are often faced with great opportunities brilliantly disguised as unsolvable problems." He's right, and there are two great opportunities that I encounter regularly as a parent.

The First Great Opportunity: Time

I am too busy, nearly all the time. My work is demanding, and the activities and obligations of a five-person family keep us all endlessly on the go. My own acid test: if I am too busy to spend time with my kids, I'm too busy. I changed my goal from being purposeful to just being with my kids in direct response to being too busy.

The momentum of constant activity from the workday can carry into the evening and into the weekend too, and with it the expectation of being productive. It may not be productive to play outside after dinner with my kids, but it is wonderfully meaningful to all of us. I want to be with and appreciate them while they are here, because, before we know it, they will be off and out on their own. That is how it is and how it should be. That is how God planned it, but I miss them in advance when I think about it.

So when our girls want to play catch or be pushed on the swing, or our son wants to play cards or watch a movie with me, what am I to say, "I'm too busy?" With what? This is my life and theirs, and if I am too busy, I will miss it and them. Part of our solution to this is that we have family night each week. We play games, watch a movie or get together with another family. We do a lot together as a family, from Scouts to soccer, and I am continually looking for ways to simplify our lives and to free up more time to be together.

The Second Great Opportunity: Temper

I think this is perhaps every parent's greatest challenge, or at least it's mine: keeping my temper when my kids act up. I find it frustrating to ask a child to start or stop doing something over and over and over again in the space of a few minutes. You may have friends who face similar challenges. Please visit us at beforewesaygoodnight.com/keepcool if you have some words of wisdom on how to stay centered and keep your cool with your kids. This is what works best for us:

- Getting enough sleep. We often feel under-rested, but when we do get enough rest, we are better parents. Rest includes downtime to just read or relax.
- Meditation restores and revives us.
- Exercise, a great stress reliever, increases our energy to keep up with the kids.
- Date night gives us a breather as a couple and reminds us that having children was not the only reason we got married.

- Date weekend, harder to come by but immensely renewing and restorative.
- In *1-2-3 Magic,* Thomas Phelan, Ph.D., teaches a simple and effective method to calmly get your kids (under twelve) to do what you ask them to do without getting upset.
- *ScreamFree Parenting: The Revolutionary Approach to Raising Your Kids by Keeping Your Cool,* by Hal Edward Runkel. This book is another invaluable resource which promotes the idea that as parents we need to keep calm when our kids lose their cool. By being responsible for our behavior with them, we teach them by example to be responsible for their behavior.
- In Help--My Kid Is Driving Me Crazy, David Swanson, Psy.D., identifies 17 manipulative behaviors children use to get their way and provides practical strategies you can use to disarm each one to curtail conflict and restore harmony at home.
- Making a conscious effort to be encouraging and kind, amazingly effective.
- Taking a timeout myself, when my patience has worn thin.
- Praying for wisdom, patience and guidance in

our parenting.

Thomas Jefferson's said, "If you are upset with someone count to ten, if you are really upset with someone count to one hundred." On the other hand, Mark Twain said, "When you're upset, count to four, when you're *really* upset, swear." Jefferson's suggestion probably works better around kids. Twain's method will increase their vocabulary.

I believe that God is loving and forgiving, and I want to be that way with my children. So how can I expect them to treat each other with kindness and respect if I am not willing to do the same? Why must they apologize to each other when they are wrong if I don't have the humility to apologize to them when I am wrong? I am the most influential man in my children's lives. Am I in charge of myself? Do I honor my commitments? Do I behave the way I want them to behave, or do I tell them how to behave and have separate rules or no rules for myself? Am I man enough to do, myself, what I ask them to do?

We meet the challenges of parenting through hard-won experience, which can make us better parents and better storytellers. I don't have it all figured out, but I have two big things going for me, my love for my family and the perseverance to never give up. And I know *that* is the secret to success in just about anything.

The Elevator

Remember my friends Kevin, Matt and Marc, who came over to our house last summer? We went swimming and Matt did the big cannonballs in the pool? They live in other parts of the country, and we get together in each person's hometown once a year to have fun and share ideas about how to do better in our work. We call that our "Study Group." We have become really good friends over the years, and we've learned a lot from one another.

Marc likes to ski, like we do. Every year he goes on a ski trip with a bunch of his other buddies, and last year he invited our study group to go along. We went to Snowmass in Colorado, which is a great ski area and, yes, I'll take you there when you're a little bit older. Yes, of course, Mama and John will come with us. Let me talk, please.

Anyhow, we had a great time skiing with Marc and his friends. There were nine of us on the trip. Since that's a big group to ski with all day, we skied in smaller groups and then met up for lunch. Every night, though, we had dinner together at some nice restaurant. A big van would arrive for us, take us to the restaurant and then bring us back to our condo. It takes quite a while for nine people to have dinner together, and one night we got back late. When the van dropped us off, we trudged through the snow to the condo and came into the lobby to the elevator. Everyone else had gone to bed, as it was late, so we had the lobby to ourselves. That was good, since nine guys standing in front of an elevator can be loud.

When the elevator door opened, we all piled in and I hit the button for the third floor, where we were staying. We started up with everyone talking and having fun, but as we passed the second floor, the elevator suddenly stopped—between the floors! It stopped dead, and there we were, all nine of us packed in like sardines in a can.

We knew no one would hear us if we yelled for help and that no one would be at the front desk if we called on the elevator phone, since it was after hours. And there was no cell signal either. So we stood there, and I had this awful sinking feeling. I imagined that we would be standing there the whole night long, and that's when I noticed the big sign at the back of the elevator. It read: "No More Than 6 Persons Allowed in the Elevator at any Time." I thought, "Great!"

Without a word, Marc started gently jumping up and down in the elevator. Now, I didn't know how to get out of an elevator when it gets stuck, but I was certain that jumping up and down was not on the list. I was about to yell, "Are you crazy?" when the elevator started moving again. In a few seconds, the door opened and we were all getting off at the third floor, just like that! In utter amazement, I asked Marc, "How did you know to do that?" And he replied, casually, as he walked toward his room, "Oh, we got stuck in there last year."

———

7

Traditions

—⚹—

Bedtime stories have become a tradition in our family, a retelling of our experience, history and values. We rarely miss a story because our kids always ask for one when I tuck them in. Sometimes I pretend I've just come in to say, "Goodnight," but they'll say, "You forgot to tell us a bedtime story!" And that makes me feel wonderful.

Girls are different from boys. You've probably noticed that too. When we found out that we were having two, at the same time, I was thrilled and a little overwhelmed. I didn't know anything about girls, just ask any of the girls I dated. How do you relate to a little girl? No idea. Then we got quite a jolt from a magazine article when we read that twins go through 9,500 diapers in the first year. We proved that point and also experienced the incredible joy, challenge and love of tripling our number of kids in one day. I remember a friend telling me, when hearing our great news, "Ah, that's *two* little fingers to wrap you around."

In the beginning, I wondered if the girls would enjoy my storytelling as much as their brother had. I'm glad to say they did, and like John, they especially enjoy stories about family members in funny situations, as in "Grandpa and the Pig."

When it comes to storytelling, gender doesn't matter. It's your story and if you tell it to your neighbor, grandmother, boy or girl of any age, your mind will automatically adjust the story to your audience. You don't have to give it any thought, it just happens.

Now, you know the work it takes to get your kids from the end of dinner to turning out the light. And though it's sometimes difficult to get two or more kids to do the same thing at the same time, there are some advantages with multiples at bedtime. So, here are some pointers on telling bedtime stories, if you have more than one child. First, any kids sharing the same room get the same story. Further, if you have kids in different rooms, you can tell the same story in each room. I won't tell if you won't. I have done this often and simply adjust the story to the age level of the listener. The story can be longer, more detailed and nuanced with older children.

Traditions helped create my own sense of family connectedness. I remember Thanksgiving at my grandparents' house and still use my grandfather's carving set for our turkey. We celebrated every fourth of July at my parents' house, with all my cousins, wildly playing Marco Polo in our pool. We'd have backyard fireworks when they were still legal and, for a while, after they weren't. Every Christmas and Easter, we'd be up at the cabin with Aunt Janice and Uncle Gordon and all my cousins skiing, building snowmen and having snowball fights. In the summer, we played flashlight tag and spent hours riding around on dirt roads in the old Model A pickup truck. I will always have those memories and enjoy sharing them with my kids. They too will have our memories together as a family, and one of them will be of their dad telling them bedtime stories as they drifted off to sleep.

Right now, *today*, is the future that I dreamed about when I was young and single: being married with a loving wife and wonderful children. Yet now that we are here, the temptation is great to get caught up in the endless rush of the world or "getting things done around the house" and miss just being together. I don't want that to be how I live my life, and storytelling is one way that I change the tide in my favor.

Telling stories and reading aloud to our children offer the complementary benefits of inspiring their imagination and their love of reading. Speaking at Parent's Night, our girls' school librarian said, "There is a time when you stop reading to your children and they start reading to you. Children need to internalize a narrative voice, and if you're lucky it will be yours." Reading to our children and telling stories give us two opportunities to be that voice.

Now I can really influence them, so I need to take advantage of that and build a bond that will withstand the onslaught of the teen years. This is my chance and it will never be here again. Tucking my girls in the other night I asked, "Why do you like bedtime stories?" And one replied, "Because I use my imagination when you're telling the stories." And I began to say, "Once upon a time," and the other stopped me and said, "I want to hear a real story about your life." And that made my day.

Love, Marriage and Gizmo

Shortly after Mama and I first met, I went over to her townhouse to pick her up for our second date and got a rude surprise. She had a black cat, a Burmese which I immediately disliked. My impression was that the feeling was mutual. I can't remember why I didn't like Gizmo, but I do remember wondering if Mama and I were going to hit it off, because I did not like that cat. I was a dog guy, and that cat had a "Who the heck are you? And what are you doing in my house?" sort of attitude. After meeting Gizmo, I was wondering that myself.

Somehow I was able to put Gizmo out of my mind. And we sort of put up with each other, as Mom and I dated, fell in love and got married; that is, until Mom moved into my place when we got back from our honeymoon and Gizmo moved in with her.

Oh, she liked the house alright and seemed to get along okay with Winston, though I think he pretty much ignored her. We stayed out of each other's way and took a live-and-let-live approach to being under the same roof. But one night, early in our marriage, I was lying in bed reading and noticed something. We were about to turn out the lights, and I saw that there were a few fine black hairs on my pillowcase. Somehow in the next moment, there seemed to be one in my mouth and I was hopping mad about it. I complained to Mom, who looked at me like I was a little crazy and perhaps was wondering if her thirty-day money-back guarantee on me was still in effect. I could see her doing the mental calculations.

Somehow we survived all that, and Gizmo and I gradually got used to each other and even grew to like each other, a little bit. After a while, I enjoyed her jumping up in my lap to be petted and meowing at me in the morning and when I came home from work. Do you know what I liked best? I liked having her up on the bed at night, as I read. I would pull up the covers a little bit and make a little cave, where she would crawl in, turn around and lie right next to me and purr. I had fallen in love with Gizmo, just like I had with Mama.

Gizmo's gone now, but I have a picture of her in my office at home, lying on a red pillow on the sofa in our den. She became part of our family and was there when you were born. She was a wonderful cat, though it took me a while to realize it. And I still miss her.

——— —— ——

8

Building Bridges

"I aspire to be as good a man as my dog thinks I am."

THOMAS JEFFERSON

—⚉—

Now that our son is a teenager, we ask ourselves, how did that happen? It seems not long ago when he was two and I began telling him bedtime stories. Every parent will tell you that the time goes by quickly, and it does. As our son has become more independent, a new benefit of storytelling has emerged. All those hours together led to many conversations, away from bedtime, about nearly everything. We have developed a habit of communicating that would not be as strong as it is, without the bedtime stories we shared. We talk about life in general, from politics to technology, history and the future, and, at great length, about the idea that fourteen-year-olds should have complete and unbridled freedom, with barely any parental supervision.

The great benefit of our continuing conversations is that I know what my son wants in his life and what his hopes and dreams are. That doesn't mean we never argue or have a perfect relationship. But we do know how to talk with each other, because we have done that nearly every day of his life. Boys need their fathers as the example of what it means to be a man and how to be one. Girls need their fathers too, in order to learn how to relate to men in emotionally healthy ways and how to spot a good one and avoid the bad ones.

We love our kids and want them to know it, but we don't coddle them either. Our kids think we're stricter than any of their friends' parents, or at least they tell us we are. I haven't done a survey, but I expect that many of their friends use the same line on their parents. It's fairly simple, with responsibility and maturity come privileges, not the other way around. Our kids will grow up physically and become adults *no matter what we do*. Whether they become capable adults with good values and character has a lot to do with what we do as parents. And Liz and I know that how we relate with each other and them is *the* model of marriage and good behavior that our kids will most carry with them throughout their lives.

As our kids get older, there will be more stories to tell them, my grandfather's experiences in the trenches of France in World War I and later as a federal judge in Washington D.C., *their* grandfather's experiences in World War II and his wild youth. They'll hear more of the incredible influence my grandmothers, aunts and mother have had on my life. The depth of the stories and the details expand exponentially with the age of your child. This is one of the reasons you will never run out of material. As our son has become older, I tell him more about present-day experiences too, and we have graduated from G to PG to PG13 material.

As parents, we tend to think of our kids as always having been here, at their current age, and always remaining with us as kids. The reality is that they and we are always transitioning toward the future. Rather than try to hold back the tide, I want to help them grow up and mentor them toward their adulthood. Older kids may not want to hear a bedtime story, but this is an opportunity to transition to conversation covering nearly anything. And you can always sneak in a story on a walk, in the car or at dinner. I see storytelling as a foundation on which to build an ongoing way of relating to one another. It's a bridge to my children's future and to our future together.

The Bet

When I was about nineteen, I was over at Uncle Stephen's house one Friday night, hanging out with him, Uncle Johnny, Uncle Scott and a few of our other friends. As usual, we were listening to loud music, telling jokes, watching TV, playing poker and eating pizza, all at the same time. None of us were married yet, not even close, and we were arguing and talking about all the usual things guys of that age discuss: girls, cars, movies, music, concerts, and school. Oh yeah, we were also talking about how to *meet* girls. As the night wore on, we played poker of every variety: Texas hold 'em, five-card draw, Jacks are wild, you get the idea.

At some point, we started talking about physical prowess and about who could or couldn't do what, pull-ups, sit-ups, kick the top of the doorway, etc. I announced that I could take the plastic top-piece that holds together a six-pack of soda and fold it over upon itself until it became one single plastic circle the width of a soda can. I claimed that I could wrap the plastic circle over my two big toes, stand on my head and break it apart using only the strength of my feet. Not quite Houdini, but it got their attention.

Uncle Stephen didn't believe this idiotic idea for a second and immediately bet me ten thousand dollars that I couldn't do it. I accepted. They ran to get a soda-can holder, and I took off my shoes and socks to prepare myself for the challenge. Limbering up and stretching, I took some deep breaths. Then, carefully, I folded the cover into one circle the size of a soda can. The crowd tensed as I sat on the floor and put the plastic over my toes. Then the room drew deathly quiet. I closed my eyes and took several meditative breaths then leaned forward and pulled myself into a headstand, which is pretty easy to do if you use your forearms to support yourself. They watched my toes and waited. And with one powerful move, I broke the plastic apart. The crowd went wild! Congratulations all around. You might be wondering what about the ten thousand dollars? I didn't collect it, a fact that I remind Uncle Stephen of from time to time. It was kind of a silly bet anyway.

Knowing that I could do it was satisfaction enough, and I knew I could, since earlier in the day I already had done it... twice.

9

Share Your Treasure

"Do what you can with what you have,
where you are."

THEODORE ROOSEVELT

—w—

You **are the door** to your children's family history, and their opportunity to hear it relies upon you to tell it to them. This is a great treasure, though they may not realize it because of all the competing noise. We know that all history, before the written word, was passed down orally through stories, music and art. Yet don't you find it ironic that, as we have become more and more advanced in our ability to communicate in a myriad of electronic ways, our ability to simply relate person-to-person seems to have diminished? Storytelling is an opportunity to beat the competing noise and relate more deeply with one another.

Nothing compares with your children's memories of *you* telling them your story. There is something in the telling of a story that transcends the written version of it. Perhaps it is simply that it is you telling it and your children listening to it. Whatever it is, it can be a beautiful experience that your children cannot get enough of.

Our children learn our values, skills and wisdom through their experience of being with us. We pass on these treasures, directly and indirectly, at all times. We enhance the gradual transfer of this treasure when we add storytelling to our way of being with our kids. When we share the story of our experience, we impart the richness of our values and hard-won wisdom to our children without even trying. Our children receive this heritage as a bonus while enjoying the story and the time together.

How often have you heard it said that it's time to interview Mom or Dad because they know so much more about the family than anyone else. And when they're gone, so are the stories that only they knew. And yet how many people do we know who actually have interviewed their family members and recorded their stories? Telling your story to your children as bedtime stories is an opportunity for connecting deeply with your children and passing on to them an invaluable treasure, your family history. You might even say it's priceless.

This is not a test, but it is your life. You will not be graded or recorded, except in your children's memory. What do you want your legacy to be with your children, and what treasure will you leave them?

How would you like to do something to help other children, to share a little of your treasure with them? Two out of three people go to sleep each night without enough food to eat. There are nearly one billion people on the planet who cannot read. Though many other factors play a role, there is a clear and direct connection between illiteracy, poverty and hunger. It doesn't have to stay that way, and you can help to change it.

Have you heard of John Wood? He has quite a story to tell. John was a highly successful executive for Microsoft. In fact, he was in charge of business development in China. Then after a life-changing backpacking trip to Nepal, he gave it all up to start a charitable, nonprofit organization. *Room to Read* helps children in the developing world break the cycle of poverty by providing access to educational resources. Since the year 2000, *Room to Read* has donated millions of books, established over 9,000 libraries and nearly 1,200 schools, published 433 new local-language children's books and supported the education of over 8,700 girls in countries throughout Asia and Africa. Reading is a critical step forward on the road out of poverty, and kids who learn to read will teach their children to read when they become parents. John Wood left Microsoft to change the world and is doing so one book at a time. To find out how you can help, visit www. roomtoread.org.

There is a story of a young man walking down a deserted beach. In the distance, he sees a figure coming toward him. As he gets closer, he notices that it is an old man who bends over every few steps, picks up something and throws it into the ocean. The young man is curious and, as the old man gets closer, he sees that he is throwing starfish back into the ocean. The young man asks, "What are you doing?" And the old man replies, "I'm throwing starfish back into the ocean." The young man asks, "Why? There are hundreds of starfish on this beach. What possible difference can it make?" The old man reaches down, picks up another starfish and throws it back into the ocean, saying, "It made a difference to that one."

No one can do everything, but everyone can do something.

Trail Riding

When Aunt Janice lived in Georgia, she had to leave her horses behind in Los Angeles. So Grammy and Grandpa would go out to the stables where the horses were boarded to ride them now and then. They would take the horses out on the trails through Griffith Park, the largest park in Los Angeles.

One afternoon, Grammy and Grandpa went to the stables, brushed and saddled the horses and headed out. The trail went through a tunnel under the freeway and led into Griffith Park. Meandering along for several miles, Grammy and Grandpa had a nice day of riding. After a while, they decided it would be best to head back, as it was getting late in the afternoon and would take some time to return to the stables and put away the horses.

The ride back was uneventful until they came back to the trail leading to the tunnel under the freeway. For some reason, Grandpa's horse got spooked and took off at a gallop down the trail in the direction of a sharp turn before the tunnel. A galloping horse can't make a sharp turn, and this horse was wild with fear and completely out of control.

To make matters *a lot worse*, as Grandpa pulled back hard on the reins to try to slow down the horse, the reins broke! So there he was, on an out-of-control horse galloping toward a brick wall with no way to stop. I'll tell you the rest of the story tomorrow night. (*All* the Frazees are teasers, and I couldn't resist saying that. Once the protests died down, I continued.)

Okay, let's see, where was I? Oh yeah, so there's Grandpa on a runaway horse, galloping toward a wall, with broken reins and no way to stop. Now that's trouble...unless you grew up spending time on your grandfather's farm, in the middle of Kansas, and knew a lot about horses and how to ride, and luckily Grandpa had and did.

When he saw what was coming, Grandpa leaned way out over the neck of his horse and gently covered the horse's eyes with his hands. And the horse stopped. When the horse could no longer see where he was going, he stopped. And do you know what? Some people will tell you that horses are dumb…but they're not stupid.

10

Story Prompters

"To keep a lamp burning,
we have to keep putting oil in it."

MOTHER TERESA

—⚹—

The crucial first element in telling a good story is deciding who or what to tell the story about. You must begin with people or animals as your characters, for without them you have no story. And the characters must be engaged in an experience or taking some kind of action. When you have that, you have the basis for a story. Now the reality is that you have thousands of stories to tell, but they're sometimes hard to remember on the spur of the moment. You need access to the hard drive of your memory.

That's why I invented Story Prompters, included at the end of this chapter, to provide a simple way to access an endless supply of stories to tell. You can use them to have a story ready in advance or to prompt a story on the spot, the way I do. The point is to tell a good story. Whether you have one ready or want to be more spontaneous in your telling makes no difference. It's really a matter of personal style and preference.

The first bedtime stories that I told were about me. As I went along, I realized that I could greatly expand my repertoire if I included other family members and friends as the subjects of the stories. Story Prompters helped me to access those memories. I just ran through my experiences and family history and a story would pop up. I did not have a written list, but it always worked to access the memories in my mind. So when I decided to write this book, I wanted to give you something you could easily review to prompt a story, especially if you are new at this.

Do you know what's great about our memories and experiences? If you can remember them, your stories will be entertaining; but if they're not, you won't remember them. That seems to be the way our brains work. If you'd like a little extra security in this process, do the following:

- Create a story notebook on your cell phone or tablet or buy a small notebook for your car, office and home.

- When you think of a memory or experience during the day, write it down in your story notebook. You don't need to include details. Simply give it a title, such as "Grandpa and the Pig."

- Cruise through the Story Prompters, on the

following pages, and make a list of story titles that interest you, for future use.

- Ask your family for their memories and experiences. You might share this book with them and compare notes. They will likely have experiences that you haven't heard about and some you've forgotten too.

- Look through your photo albums and pictures. Home movies are a good source of stories too. Write down possible story titles, as these images will bring back memories.

Remember, you don't have to write a story. You only need to think of a memory or experience and write down a title. Be sure to write it down, as there is a tendency to forget the idea between when you think of it and when you want to tell it. When you sit down to tell the story later that evening, you'll be able to tell it without any notes or rehearsal, even if you've never told it before. We will discuss the details of how to structure a story in the next chapter.

The Story Prompters are presented as two lists divided into categories for ease of reference: people and animals on the left-facing page and places, experiences and things on the right-facing page. The lists are designed to be cross-referenced with each other to prompt a story. Look at the list of people and animals on the left-facing page, choose one or two as your subject and combine it with an item or two from the list of places, experiences and things on the right-facing page to prompt your memory for stories to tell.

For example, the first story in this book, "A Hot Breakfast," is about my mother, sister and me (people) and took place in our kitchen (place) at breakfast when I was two and a half (when), with the toaster and table (things). Notice how each additional detail brings the story more into focus. You want to have a character or characters at a specific time, engaging in a specific experience or action. In reviewing these lists, you will remember experiences in your life and stories from your family.

As you will see, Story Prompters can provide a nearly unlimited number of ideas for a story. Consulting the lists prior to storytelling, or simply bringing them to mind, as you are about to begin, is fine. Both approaches work, and it gets easier with practice. If you feel more comfortable having a story in mind before you come into the room, feel free to do that. As you get used to telling stories, you may find the adventuresome approach of coming up with them on the spot, without reference to the lists, more exciting. Once you begin talking, the story will unfold. After all, you know the subject and the experience or event and just have to tell what happened.

Here's another way to put it. Choose one or more of the characters from the people and animals list on the left and focus on it to remind you of a place, experience or thing from the list on the right. For example, if you select yourself as a child in school, there are multiple possibilities that may come to mind. Throw in a sibling or a friend, or two, and you have dozens of possibilities. By combining multiple people and experiences, you increase your options exponentially. The following is a list of possible combinations, with examples of stories from this book, but you can use any combination so long as it leads you to a story you and your kids will enjoy.

- You and an animal: "Winston"

- You and other people (family members) and an experience: "A Hot Breakfast"

- You and other people (cousins) and selections from multiple categories (summer vacation, bugs

and snakes, things you did for fun as a kid):
"Snakes and Bumblebees"

- Other people (family) and an experience (horseback riding): "Trail Riding"

- Other people (family) with other people (a helpful stranger) and an experience (shopping): "Christmas Shopping"

- Other people (cousins) with other people (family) and selections from multiple categories (family vacations, practical jokes): "Magic Fingers"

Story Prompters

Choose the character(s) and the experience

You can mix and match from the following Story-Prompter combinations. These lists are set up to easily cross-reference most of the people you know, with multiple categories. Just remember, paraphrasing Thomas Edison, when you think you've exhausted every possibility, you haven't. An additional advantage of Story Prompters is that you can use them to interview your family members to fill in your family history. Please note that the People and Animals page is repeated on each of the left-facing pages that follow, while the right-facing pages are a continuation of the much longer list needed for the categories of Places, Experiences and Things. Please visit beforewesaygoodnight.com/storyprompters for additional story prompter ideas and to add your own suggestions to our ever growing list of Story Prompters.

PEOPLE AND ANIMALS

FAMILY
You and your spouse
Your kids
Brothers and sisters
Parents and grandparents
Aunts, uncles and cousins
Nieces and nephews
Other family members
Great-grandparents
Ancestors

ROLE MODELS, LEADERS
Those who influenced you
Your heroes
Favorite teachers
Scout leaders
Coaches and mentors
Sports heroes
Camp counselors

OTHER PEOPLE
Artists and writers
The dentist or doctor
The police or firefighters
Other interesting people
Shop/business owners

FRIENDS
Best friends, then & now
Other friends, then & now
Neighbors, then & now
Your friends' families
Your parents' friends
Pen pals

ANIMALS
Your cats or dogs
Pet tricks
Horses and farm animals
Small and large pets
Unusual pets
Family and friends' pets
Wild animals

TIME PERIODS AND ERAS
Infants and toddlers
You or your spouse as...
    a kid and in your teens,
    in your 20's to 90's, etc.
Relatives at these ages
Friends at these ages
Your favorite age

PLACES, EXPERIENCES AND THINGS

ACCOMPLISHMENTS
Awards, degrees, honors
Challenges
What you're proud of

CARS
Family cars
Favorite cars
First car, worst car
Learning to drive
Riding in the car

CHILDHOOD HOME
Front and back yard
Bedrooms and den
Kitchen and dining room
Living and family room
Garage or basement
The street you grew up on
Neighborhood and town

DAILY LIFE
Allowance and chores
Backyard barbeques
Bedtime and bath time
Bikes and learning to ride
Candy and snacks
Cell phones, computers

Clothes
Earliest remembrance
Funny experiences
Games, toys and dolls
Meals, cooking and food
Restaurants and shopping
Skateboards & blades
TV, video games, radio
Weekends and weather

FAITH
Childhood experiences
Childhood prayers
Ceremonies & celebrations
Religious holidays
Your faith

FAMILY HISTORY
Birthplace and genealogy
Family legends and stories
Names and nicknames
Country of origin

FAMILY TRADITIONS
Parties and presents
Celebration traditions
Heritage and customs

PEOPLE AND ANIMALS

FAMILY
You and your spouse
Your kids
Brothers and sisters
Parents and grandparents
Aunts, uncles and cousins
Nieces and nephews
Other family members
Great-grandparents
Ancestors

ROLE MODELS, LEADERS
Those who influenced you
Your heroes
Favorite teachers
Scout leaders
Coaches and mentors
Sports heroes
Camp counselors

OTHER PEOPLE
Artists and writers
The dentist or doctor
The police or firefighters
Other interesting people
Shop/business owners

FRIENDS
Best friends, then & now
Other friends, then & now
Neighbors, then & now
Your friends' families
Your parents' friends
Pen pals

ANIMALS
Your cats or dogs
Pet tricks
Horses and farm animals
Small and large pets
Unusual pets
Family and friends' pets
Wild animals

TIME PERIODS AND ERAS
Infants and toddlers
You or your spouse as...
  a kid and in your teens,
  in your 20's to 90's, etc.
Relatives at these ages
Friends at these ages
Your favorite age

PLACES, EXPERIENCES AND THINGS

FAVORITES
Books, poems, and songs
Candy, desserts, ice cream
Other foods
Jokes and funny stories
Music, songs, bands
Sports to play or watch

HOBBIES AND INTERESTS
Crafts and model building
Dance, theatre and ballet
Drawing and painting
Gardening, growing food
Music, singing and lessons
Reading and writing
Collecting

HOLIDAYS
Civic and religious
Holiday memories
New Year's Eve
Valentine's Day
The Fourth of July
Halloween and costumes
Thanksgiving

HOPES AND DREAMS
Adventures to have
Dream home or trip
Dreams of childhood
Places to go, people to see

OUTDOOR FUN
Backpacking and camping
Beaches and deserts
Boats, off-road vehicles
Farms and ranches
Fishing and hunting
Mountains, lakes, rivers
Skiing, surfing, swimming
Snorkeling, scuba diving

PARENTS AND GRANDPARENTS
Their life experiences
Times with your parents
Where they grew up
How they met
Military service
Stories they told you
Their work
Their likes and dislikes
What they taught you

PEOPLE AND ANIMALS

FAMILY
You and your spouse
Your kids
Brothers and sisters
Parents and grandparents
Aunts, uncles and cousins
Nieces and nephews
Other family members
Great-grandparents
Ancestors

ROLE MODELS, LEADERS
Those who influenced you
Your heroes
Favorite teachers
Scout leaders
Coaches and mentors
Sports heroes
Camp counselors

OTHER PEOPLE
Artists and writers
The dentist or doctor
The police or firefighters
Other interesting people
Shop/business owners

FRIENDS
Best friends, then & now
Other friends, then & now
Neighbors, then & now
Your friends' families
Your parents' friends
Pen pals

ANIMALS
Your cats or dogs
Pet tricks
Horses and farm animals
Small and large pets
Unusual pets
Family and friends' pets
Wild animals

TIME PERIODS AND ERAS
Infants and toddlers
You or your spouse as...
    a kid and in your teens,
    in your 20's to 90's, etc.
Relatives at these ages
Friends at these ages
Your favorite age

PLACES, EXPERIENCES AND THINGS

SCHOOL EXPERIENCES
Preschool
Elementary, middle school
High school and college
School days and friends
Favorite & worst teachers
Favorite subjects & grade
Homework and field trips
Getting to school
School buses

SPORTS AND RECREATION
Baseball and basketball
Football and track
Ice skating and hockey
Horseback riding
Ping pong and pool
School & spectator sports
Racquet sports
Water and snow skiing

TRAVEL
Best family vacation
Camping
Cruises
Farthest destination

WORK
Your work
Your spouse's work
Your parents' work
Best and worst bosses
Best and worst jobs
First and hardest jobs
Every job you've ever had

YOU AND YOUR SPOUSE
How you met
Your first and other dates
Meeting your in-laws
Getting engaged
Your wedding day
Honeymoon
Your first home
Having children

YOUR KIDS
The day they were born
As a baby
Bath time and bedtime
Favorite memories of them
First words, first steps
Favorite toys and foods
What they were like

Mr. Armstrong's Gift

When I was a kid, we had a handyman whose name was Horace Armstrong. As far as I can remember, no one ever called him Horace. All the kids and adults called him Mr. Armstrong. For quite a while, it didn't even occur to me that he had a first name. But I liked saying his name, Mr. Armstrong. It sounded solid and dependable.

Everyone in our family, and a lot of our friends' families, hired him to build and fix things around the house. Mr. Armstrong lived near us on a farm-like property that's not there anymore. We would sometimes go over with Grandpa to visit him. He kept chickens and ducks for fresh eggs, as many people did back then. We chased the chickens, and the ducks chased us.

I always enjoyed his workshop the most, which was right behind his house in the shade of two large oak trees. It had a faded, been-there-a-million-years look to it, with its peeling, multicolored paint and tattered roof. Inside, the workshop was always a mess, with lots of weird tools scattered about. It was hard to imagine what some of those tools were used for, but I knew that Mr. Armstrong knew what to do with them. That's because Mr. Armstrong could build *anything*. You name it, cabinets, chairs, tables, storage buildings, fences, gates, walls, windows, doors, anything.

He could also fix anything. I won't give you the list, but if it was broken he could fix it. And if he built it, it couldn't be broken because Mr. Armstrong built things to last. Everything he built was solid and dependable, just like him, and was glued and screwed and clamped and bracketed together. You couldn't break it if you tried, and occasionally, being kids, we did try.

Mr. Armstrong was about one hundred and fifty years old and so was his wife, or at least they seemed that old to me. I don't remember much about Mrs. Armstrong, other than that she was large and friendly and baked homemade pies. She would give us a slice of pie with a glass of milk when we visited. The Armstrongs were just good, plain folks.

In my memory, Mr. Armstrong was always dressed in grey overalls and a long-sleeved plaid shirt with the sleeves turned up. His hair seemed to stand straight up and was grey with some red in it. His skin was covered with freckles upon freckles. He had coarse reddish hair on his forearms and could lift or carry anything by himself and rarely asked anyone for help in any way. In fact, he hardly spoke at all and, when he did, his voice sounded garbled and fairly unintelligible to me, and he was quite hard of hearing. He was somewhat gruff and hurried in his demeanor and wore a scowl on his face a good part of the time. Nonetheless, his appearance didn't mean anything, and we knew it. If something struck him as funny, he had a wonderful smile that would slowly creep over his face, like the sun coming up in the morning.

Mr. Armstrong was also generous and kind and would often give us a toy which he'd made himself, a truck, a plane, or a puzzle. Each of these gifts were made of wood by his rough hands and given without ceremony. He just did it out of kindness, for all of us.

Now, I know that you have seen men working on the roads. Sometimes they have giant spools of cable lined up in a row. They dig long trenches in the road to lay the cable in, or string it overhead for phone or power lines. Anyway, one day, Mr. Armstrong brought one of those giant spools over to our house in his old work truck.

The wheel, as we came to call it, looked exactly like one of those giant spools on the outside, because, in fact, that's what it was. It stood about five-feet tall. Mr. Armstrong had replaced the insides with something totally amazing. He built seating for two riders opposite and upside down to each other, with their backs against the inside of the outside wall of the wheel. Climbing in on one side, I sat on the bench seat facing the center, with a place for my feet and a bar to hold onto. Mr. Armstrong rolled the wheel a half turn, which turned me upside down, and Aunt Mary Ellen crawled into the other side. We were now seated and laughing wildly. Looking through the bars, all we saw were each other's feet. And when we moved, the wheel rolled, with us inside.

You know we lived on a fairly level cul-de-sac. There were about twenty kids living in our neighborhood, and in about two minutes of hearing about the wheel, the other eighteen were in front of our house begging for a ride. We were out there until dark that day and many days after that. We discovered that several kids could act as guides for the wheel, while others rode inside. The riders would come out dizzy and elated as can be after their turn. Once their heads stopped spinning, they would take over as guides and work their way back to another turn in the wheel.

I remember Mr. Armstrong standing there with my dad, and what happiness he brought the day he brought the wheel over. The wheel became the most popular attraction in our neighborhood. It was like having a carnival ride in your own yard, and we played in it until we were all too big to fit anymore. When that happened, we gave it to some family friends with smaller kids, as Mr. Armstrong had done for us. Maybe it's still out there somewhere, rolling around, with kids getting dizzy and having fun. I'd like to think so, for that was one of the nicest things anyone has ever done for me. And I'd like to say again, "Thanks, Mr. Armstrong."

11

Mildly to Wildly Entertaining

"Laughter is the shortest distance between two people."

VICTOR BORGE

—∞—

Once you have chosen the character(s) and experience, using Story Prompters or any other method, you need to build a structure around your story. You don't have to create the world's greatest short story, so relax. We're simply talking about telling a two- to five-minute story to your kids at bedtime. The guidelines listed below will show you how to form a structure within the story, which will make it easy to tell and entertaining to listen to. The structure is the natural framework of a good story. Any story will have these elements. These guidelines will help to make sure you're on the right track.

The good news is that you already know how to tell a story. Surprised? In reality, we tell stories all the time. A story is simply your description of an experience you've had. Think about the last time you received a traffic ticket. If you told someone about it, notice that your description had all the elements listed below without your even thinking about it. This is naturally how we relate our experiences to one another. You can do the same thing in telling a bedtime story. If you choose a subject you are interested in and simply narrate what happened, you will tell a good story.

Here are some specific guidelines I use to tell bedtime stories. You'll see that there is a difference between just reciting the facts and telling a story. Use these steps to check that your stories are indeed stories. Every good story has three key elements: the character(s), the structure and the use of the reporter's motto. Now let's look at how you can apply the same three-step method to telling your children the story of your life and family.

The Character(s)

Use Story Prompters, or any other method that works for you, to choose the people or animals which will be the real-life characters in your story. Choosing the character(s) is the first step toward telling a good bedtime story. It's worth repeating that the character(s) must be engaged in an action or experience. Use your story notebook if you are new to storytelling. Keeping your list of story titles handy and adding to it, when a story comes to mind, will take the stress out of this part of the equation.

The Structure

A good story has three parts: a beginning, middle and an end. Think of any fairy tale, movie or children's story, and you will see that this is so. What do "Jack and the Beanstalk," *Star Wars* and *Green Eggs and Ham* all have in common? They all have a beginning, middle and an end, of course. Visualize your character(s) having an experience within this three-part structure, and you are two-thirds of the way toward telling a great bedtime story.

The Reporter's Motto

The third part of telling an engaging story fits neatly inside of the structure. It's been referred to as "the reporter's motto" and answers the questions of who, what, where, when, why and how. Reporters use this method to remind themselves to include these descriptive elements in their news stories. This works well for a bedtime story too.

Just think of it this way: the beginning tells your listeners *who* the story is about and *where* and *when* it happened. The middle tells them *what* happened. The end tells them *how* the story concludes.

You may be wondering what happened to the *why*. The *why* can be in the beginning, middle, end or in all three. The *why* is the reason that the events in the story happened. For example, in "Snakes and Bumblebees," the *why* is revealed in the beginning by kids looking for ways to entertain themselves on a summer's day. In "A Hot Breakfast," the *why* shows up in the middle with a faulty toaster. Waiting until the end to reveal the *why* can make a story more humorous, as in "The Elevator." Marc's casual revelation, "We got stuck in there last year," implies the *why* of the story. The *why* of "Mr. Armstrong's Gift" is the kindness of an old man toward children and weaves its way throughout the story. It's really up to you and the story as to where *why* ends up. I don't consciously put the *why* into any of the stories. The *why* knows its way around and will usually find a place where it's comfortable. You don't need to give much thought to it.

Check out any of the stories in this book or think about any story you've ever heard, and you will see that they all follow these guidelines. As you read them, notice that whether the stories are short or long, they work because they each have at least one character in an experience or taking some kind of action. They have a beginning, middle and end and answer the basic questions of who, what, where, when, why and how, all the ingredients of a good story. I promise you, if your stories have these elements, they will work. Put another way, if you follow the recipe for chocolate cake, you're not going to end up with meatloaf.

And the great news is that you already know how to do this! Let me prove it to you. Let's revisit the unfortunate subject of your getting that traffic ticket. If you recall the time you told that story, it had structure: a beginning, middle and end. And you, no doubt, threw in all of the details of the reporter's motto, who, what, where, when, how and probably why, with great detail and drama. Yes, it is possible that your version of why you got the ticket differs somewhat from the police officer's version. But let's stay on track, and let me ask you a question or two. Did you have to stop and think about the structural elements when you told that story? Or did you tell it as quickly as the words spilled out? You see? You already know how to tell a good story. The guidelines above are here simply to help you keep on track. And remember, please drive safely.

Now that you have the basics down, here are some additional thoughts to keep in mind as you progress in telling bedtime stories to your kids. Remember, you're not aiming for a Pulitzer Prize. This is just you, your kids and your memories.

Choose a Story You Are Interested In!

The most important tip in storytelling is to be engaged in telling the story. Here's a test. If I think it's boring, I guarantee my kids will think it's incredibly boring. I start by choosing a story that I'm interested in or find entertaining. Goofy, strange or funny stories are always winners. Personal stories that let them see what I was like as a kid are particularly fascinating to them. After they got over the initial shock that I actually was a kid, they have really enjoyed getting to know that kid. I also think the bedtime stories about me ease the pressure on them of feeling like they have to be perfect. I wasn't. They see that I made plenty of mistakes. Yet I still somehow managed to limp into adulthood and turned out all right. They can relate to me more easily, and it gives me a much needed reminder that they are not little adults, as I sometimes expect them to be. They are kids and they think and behave like kids.

Be Genuine and Have Fun!

Laugh with your kids and be yourself. Not every story is going to be funny, but they can be entertaining to listen to and to tell. Enjoy the story and the "goodnights" that happen afterwards.

You may be quiet or animated, or in between. The whole experience is fun for everyone.

Use Your Voice

Be dramatic. If the story calls for an amazed or conspiratorial tone, go for it. I don't overdo it, but I do get into the story. If it's about an old or unusual character, I change my voice to fit the character. If it's a story of discovery or suspense, I'm there. Look at it this way, if Dakota Fanning can star in a movie, I can add a little drama to my kids' bedtime stories.

No Criticism, Tone or Lectures

Be patient with them and yourself. Luckily, at bedtime, I have a fairly easy time with this one. Regardless of how challenging the day has been for me or with them, when the lights go out I have no problem keeping my cool. The instructional period of the day is over.

The point is this. When my kids are grown and thinking back about how it was having me as their dad, how do I want them to remember their time with me? I know they'll remember plenty of fun times and plenty of times when I got mad at them. I'd like to think that I'm more patient and kind than impatient and gruff.

Of one thing I'm sure, and that is that my kids will have fond memories of our time together each night, when I told them of my adventures and those of their family. The magic just happens when you tell a bedtime story, and it will work for you too.

Too Short /Too Late/Too Long

If I'm uninspired and just want to get to sleep, I will sometimes try to get away with a really short story. Believe me, I've tried it all. Watch out for this in your own storytelling. Short stories don't work if they lack a beginning, middle or end. Without this structure, a story has no point and isn't really a story at all, but merely a statement of facts. This is almost always the result of being tired or not having a subject in mind and trying to fake your way out of the room, so use Story Prompters and you'll do fine.

When it's late, but not too late, I do tell my kids a short story. They know these are unusual evenings and accept it without argument. At the end of this chapter, I've included three short bedtime stories that work because they have all the elements of a good story.

When it's too late or I have something else I need to do, I promise to tell them two stories the next night. That way they feel we're honoring our tradition and everybody goes to bed happy. I am truthful about the time constraints, and I keep my word the next evening, both good examples to my children.

Sometimes though we just don't get to a story on a given night but I'm always glad when we return to it.

Our kids have never complained that a story is too long and that's very telling. It underscores that they're into the story and enjoy being with me, or maybe it just beats staring at the ceiling in the dark by themselves. Or perhaps they fell asleep. And there are not many things in life better than tucking the covers around your sleeping child and kissing him or her goodnight.

Story notebook

When you think of a story your kids will find entertaining, make a title for it in your story notebook so that you will remember it later. I don't do this personally, but I endorse the practice wholeheartedly. Like carrying business cards, it's a great idea. I don't do that either, but I recommend it!

Cake

When I was a junior in high school, I had a tough science class with a teacher who was even tougher. Professor Kroose was short, bald and wore a white lab coat, with a red bow tie and black horned-rimmed glasses. You know how some people look really good bald? Well, he was one of them. Professor Kroose had a great-looking head. He looked like he was born bald. Oh, wait a second, he probably was. His voice boomed like a cannon shot, and you didn't want to be in the line of fire when he was mad.

On the first day of class, Professor Kroose handed out index cards and asked each student to write their full name and birth date on the card. When the cards were handed back in, he announced that each student would be required to bake a cake for his or her birthday. "Bring enough for everyone," he bellowed. "And bring candles, plates and forks and milk, so we can all sing 'Happy Birthday' to you." Wow! We were stunned. If your birthday fell on a weekend or holiday, he would assign you a different date to celebrate. No one was too thrilled with this, since most of the kids, including me, had never baked anything, and no one wanted to be embarrassed in front of the whole class. After a while, though, we realized that there were benefits to this arrangement; namely, that we got to have birthday cake nearly every week of the whole semester.

Professor Kroose was one of those teachers who present a tough exterior but was really a good guy once you got to know him, as long as you didn't get too far out of line. Professor Kroose had two facial expressions, stern and joyful. He loved to laugh, loudly. He did everything loudly. He was the sponsor of the ski club and took all the kids on a bus trip up to

Mammoth each year. He kept us under control, but the emphasis was on having a good time.

When my birthday came around, I went to the store with Grammy and bought three boxes of cake mix and chocolate frosting. There were over thirty students in the class, so I had a lot of cake to bake. Yet aside from a slight burn on my forearm and a little bit of lopsidedness, the cake turned out pretty well, and I had learned to bake. I kept on baking cakes, then brownies and cornbread and muffins. They filled the house with a wonderful aroma and were great to eat. Those were the only things I knew how to cook for a long time, but they sure were good, and I have Professor Kroose to thank for it. Oh, and I did learn some pretty cool stuff about science too.

Christmas Shopping

When I was a kid, the first mall in our area was Topanga Plaza, where California Pizza Kitchen is located. Grammy and her mother, my grandmother whom we called "Grama," used to do most of their Christmas shopping there, because there were so many stores to choose from. One Christmas season, they were at the mall on a particularly crowded Saturday. As Christmas was fast approaching, they were inside for several hours finishing up their shopping. When they came out, they had forgotten where they parked their car! They had arrived in Grama's green Cadillac, now nowhere to be seen. And so they searched, their arms full of bags from their shopping.

They looked around for a while and at last found the car, but could not get it opened. It was a cold day and they were getting uncomfortable standing there in the wind. A nice young man saw them and offered to help. They said they were locked out of their car. He asked them to wait a second and went to his car. Getting a wire coat hanger, he straightened it out and used it to try to open the car door.

He slid the wire between the rubber molding and the window and hooked the door lock, pulled up and "presto!" opened the car for them. They thanked him generously and he went on his way. They put the packages in the back seat and got in, shutting the doors against the cold, and put the key in the ignition—but it wouldn't turn. That's when they realized that this wasn't their car. Grammy and Grama had broken into someone else's car! Well, you can bet they got out of that car a lot faster than they had gotten in. And off they went in search of their car…again.

——— ——— ———

Nothing Hits the Spot
Like a Hamburger!

Aunt Mary and Uncle Jack lived in La Canada, near Pasadena. Aunt Dolores and Uncle John lived right behind them one street over. And when we were kids, we would "hop the fence" between their yards. Uncle Jack liked to barbeque, and, one summer evening, he was grilling hamburgers for everyone. The whole family was there enjoying themselves, including Grandpa's mother, Nonie. All the food and fixings were laid out, macaroni and potato salad, baked beans, all the good stuff you have at a barbeque.

Uncle Jack called everyone over when the burgers were ready. They went to the table and helped themselves to the salads and sides and put their burgers together. Once everyone was seated, Nonie, enjoying her dinner, said,

"Nothing hits the spot like a hamburger!" She even complimented Uncle Jack on his cooking.

A few moments later, Uncle Jack, who was still at the grill, noticed that there was one burger left. That seemed odd, so he asked if everyone had been served. That's when Nonie noticed that, while helping herself to the bun, lettuce, tomato, onion, pickles, ketchup, mustard and mayonnaise, she'd left out one item...the burger!

Everyone got a big kick out of that, including Nonie. And for years afterward, whenever we would have a family barbeque, someone would always say, "Nothin' hits the spot like a hamburger!"

——— —— ——

12

The Moral of the Story

"I would rather entertain and hope that people learned something than educate people and hope they were entertained."

WALT DISNEY

—∞—

The moral of a story is the lesson learned from an experience, and it's that wisdom that we want to pass on to our children. There is a risk, however, when it comes to moralizing in bedtime stories. It is this. We spend all day instructing our children and often all evening as well. Bedtime stories work better when they are entertaining rather than overtly instructional.

Here is what I've found. If your life reflects your values, the moral of the bedtime stories you tell will come through to your kids. Regardless of your political or religious persuasion, the moral will come through. There is a temptation to ask our kids to identify the moral of the story. If we do that, we've slipped back into the instructive mode and changed the tone in the room. It's time to give instruction a rest, it's time for rest.

Have you ever noticed that kids are more willing to let a coach, rather than their parent, show them how to throw, catch or kick a ball? This is how it works with the moral of a story too. The moral is the coach in the story. Kids understand nearly all of the subtle nuances of the stories they hear. They know who the good guys and bad guys are and what good and bad behavior is, without our pointing it out. Let the story convey the moral in a way that is subtle and naturally appealing, and kids will get it.

Notice that the lessons of fairy tales are usually self-evident too and are not expressly pointed out. For instance, what is the moral of Goldilocks and the Three Bears? Don't go into other people's houses uninvited, eat their cereal, break up their furniture and mess up their beds, especially if they are big enough to eat you. Well, that's pretty obvious. Kids are smart enough to learn as they are being entertained. The lessons can be internalized and the wisdom passed on without their even noticing it. So above all, make your bedtime stories fun for you and your kids. You and they will find it an unforgettable experience. And that is, after all, the moral of this story.

Magic Fingers

My cousin Stephen was definitely the alpha dog of our little pack, but every dog has his day as you will see. All of my cousins and I learned to drive up at the cabin in the old Model A pickup truck. We had such wonderful adventures together, all piled into the Model A, tearing around on the dirt roads, that we fell in love with that old car. So when we were old enough to get our own cars and didn't have much to spend, we all went for Model A's.

When I was about twenty, we were on one of our Model A trips with the whole family. We set out from Los Angeles to the Grand Canyon and Bryce and Zion National Parks. On the way back, we spent the night in a motel in Green River, Utah. Since there were six of us boys, we doubled up in the rooms. On this particular night, Uncle Stephen and Uncle Johnny were roommates.

When they unlocked the door to their room, Uncle Stephen went in first and noticed immediately that one of the beds had "Magic Fingers" and the other did not. He quickly claimed the "Magic Fingers" bed for himself. He was two years older than Uncle Johnny and therefore got first pick.

Now, you're probably wondering what "Magic Fingers" are. Way back when, someone invented an electrical device that, when hooked up to a bed, would cause the bed to vibrate and make it feel like you were getting a massage. Now when you think about it, if you were out on a long car trip, you might be worn out by the time you got to your motel. It would feel nice to lie down on your bed and get a massage, more or less, to help you relax and get a good night's sleep. Next to the bed was a little box, with a slot for two quarters for a fifteen-minute massage. This was also a way for the motel to make a little extra money, by offering a "Magic Fingers" massage to their guests.

So, after dropping off our bags at the motel, we headed out to dinner. I don't remember much about the dinner, but I know I'll never forget what happened afterwards. Uncle Stephen and Uncle Johnny went to their room and got in their beds. Uncle Stephen slipped two quarters into the "Magic Fingers" box and lay back to enjoy his massage. Nothing happened. He hit the machine with his hand and still nothing happened. Now Uncle Stephen is pretty handy and can fix almost anything, so he hit it again and still nothing happened.

In frustration, he climbed out of bed and began following the wire leading from the "Magic Fingers" box. And that's when he noticed that the wire was not connected to his bed. It was connected to Uncle Johnny's bed; and, further, there was Uncle Johnny happily vibrating away.

Uncle Johnny had switched the mattresses on the beds when Uncle Stephen had been out of the room. Oh, and he left the "Magic Fingers" box right next to Uncle Stephen's bed, where it had been when they first walked into the room.

You can imagine that Uncle Stephen was not too happy about his discovery! He gave Uncle Johnny quite a hard time about it or at least that's what it sounded like from down the hallway. Sometimes it's hard to tell exactly what people are saying when there's a lot of yelling going on. But I'm sure that, in the end, Uncle Johnny got a good night's sleep. After all, he had a "Magic Fingers" massage to help him relax.

Closing Thoughts

"Give a little love to a child,
and you get a great deal back."

JOHN RUSKIN

—∿—

I hope you've enjoyed reading *Before We Say "Goodnight"* and that it will help you along as you tell your own bedtime stories to your kids. Putting all of this down on paper has given me a new appreciation for my life, my family and my experiences.

The stories recounted in this book are just the tip of the iceberg of my experiences, and I know that you have countless stories of your own, as well. When you have a story in mind and a sincere desire to connect in this way with your kids, you'll be on your way. Give yourself time to get the feel of it. You'll be glad you did. God bless you and yours and happy storytelling!

We invite you to submit your favorite bedtime stories for future editions of Before We Say "Goodnight." Please go to beforewesaygoodnight .com/yourstory for story submitting guidelines.

Resources

Recommended Reading and Websites

Aesop's Fables

The Bible

Raising Resilient Children by Robert Brooks, Ph.D. and Sam Goldstein, Ph.D.

Old Mother West Wind Stories by Thornton W. Burgess

The Purpose of Boys by Michael Gurian

The Wonder of Girls by Michael Gurian

Heritage Makers, www.storybookingheritage.com (to create and publish your stories)

The Parent You Want to Be by Drs. Les and Leslie Parrott

The Last Lecture by Randy Pausch, Ph.D.

1-2-3 Magic by Thomas W. Phelan, Ph.D.

ScreamFree Parenting: The Revolutionary Approach to Raising Your Kids by Keeping Your Cool by Hal Edward Runkel

Help--My Kid Is Driving Me Crazy by David Swanson, Psy.D.

Leaving Microsoft to Change the World by John Wood

Recommended Movies and TV Shows

A Christmas Carol (PG)

"Andy of Mayberry" (G)

Back to the Future (PG)

The Bucket List (PG-13)

Evan Almighty (G)

Fireproof (PG)

Groundhog's Day (PG)

It's a Wonderful Life (G)

The Kid (PG)

Oh God (PG)

Pay It Forward (PG-13)

The Secret Life of Walter Mitty (PG)

To Kill a Mockingbird (PG-13)

Acknowledgments

It seems to me that writing a book is somewhat like building a puzzle, where the shape and number of pieces change as you progress in the writing. I haven't specifically mentioned all of my family and friends in the stories, but they are here and have influenced me and this book profoundly. For this book is in a way the story of my life. The stories and the people described here helped me to become who I am. The major influences are, of course, my family and friends, my wife and children. And these influences and this story are works in progress, much like you and your influences and your story. Someone once said, "The you you'll be ten years from now will only be made different by the books you read and the people you meet." Choose them wisely and tell your story.

I'd like to thank the following people for their help and support in bringing this book to print:

Tony D'Angelo, at www.collegiate-emowerment. org, for shining a light along the path between idea and published work. Thank you also for expanding my vision of what this book could be.

Peri Poloni-Gabriel, at www.knockoutbooks. com, for the beautiful cover design and helping us along the many steps from vision to published book.

Brandon Jeffords, at jeffordsart.blogspot.com for creating the inspired cover illustration for the book. You captured the vision and made it better than I could imagine. I would like to live in that little village, in the first house on the left.

Sharon Gibb Murdoch, Ed. D., for writing the foreword. Thank you also for your enthusiasm about the book and your passion for passing on the wisdom and experiences of families.

Kathy Cannon, my dear friend, for your encouragement and belief in this book.

Mary Frazee, my mother for your love of the book and our family stories and for always believing in me and my vision of becoming who I am, whoever that has been at any given moment throughout my life.

Randy Pausch, author of *The Last Lecture*, for inspiring me to finally write this story when he wrote, "Don't let your music die within you."

My publishers David Hancock and Rick Frishman and everyone at Morgan James, and particularly Lyza Poulin, for your enthusiasm and guidance and being so easy and fun to work with.

Terry Whalin, Acquiring Editor at Morgan James, thank you for choosing and championing my book, just as you said you would. I am forever grateful.

And especially to my wife, Liz, for your encouragement in this and in all other things, for believing in me, for giving me the time to write and for editing the book. We had a lot of fun creating *Before We Say "Goodnight,"* and countless discussions about content and structure. English, as a major in college, was one of the first things that drew us together. This book would not be what it is without your invaluable input.

About the Author

Hank Frazee grew up in California and graduated from UCLA, with a major in English Literature. An entrepreneur, he entered the life insurance business and advanced to the top one percent of insurance agents in the world. His love of family, books and words led him to write *Before We Say "Goodnight."* He lives in Los Angeles with his wife and three children and a number of cats and dogs, including Winston.

Please visit our website at

www.beforewesaygoodnight.com

We invite you to submit your favorite original bedtime stories for possible inclusion in future editions of *Before We Say "Goodnight."* Please visit beforewesaygoodnight.com/yourstory for guidelines.

We are also gathering reader's ideas for additional Story Prompters to add to our online lists. Please visit beforewesaygoodnight.com/storyprompters to make a suggestion or visitbeforewesaygoodnight. com/share to share your experiences and thoughts.

9 781614 486015